Prophets of Dissent: Essays on Maeterlinck, Strindberg, Nietzsche and Tolstoy

by
Otto Heller

Professor of Modern European Literature
in Washington University (St. Louis)

Is there a thing in this world that can be separated from the inconceivable?

> *Maeterlinck, "Our Eternity"*

KENNIKAT PRESS, INC./PORT WASHINGTON, N. Y.

To

HELLEN SEARS
staunchest of friends

PROPHETS OF DISSENT

Copyright 1918 by Alfred A. Knopf
Copyright renewed 1946 by Otto Heller
Reissued in 1968 by Kennikat Press by arrangement with
Alfred A. Knopf, Inc.

Library of Congress Catalog Card No: 68-26246
Manufactured in the United States of America

ESSAY AND GENERAL LITERATURE INDEX REPRINT SERIES

Preface

THE collocation of authors so widely at variance in their moral and artistic aims as are those assembled in this little book may be defended by the safe and simple argument that all of these authors have exerted, each in his own way, an influence of singular range and potency. By fairly general consent they are the foremost literary expositors of important modern tendencies. It is, therefore, of no consequence whether or not their ways of thinking fit into our particular frame of mind; what really matters is that in this small group of writers more clearly perhaps than in any other similarly restricted group the basic issues of the modern struggle for social transformation appear to be clearly and sharply joined. That in viewing them as indicators of contrarious ideal currents due allowance must be made for peculiarities of temperament, both individual and racial, and, correspondingly, for the purely "personal equation" in their spiritual attitudes, does not detract to any material degree from their generic significance.

Preface

In any case, there are those of us who in the vortical change of the social order through which we are whirling, feel a desire to orient ourselves through an objective interest in letters among the embattled purposes and policies which are now gripped in a final test of strength. In a crisis that makes the very foundations of civilization quake, and at a moment when the salvation of human liberty seems to depend upon the success of a united stand of all the modern forces of life against the destructive impact of the most primitive and savage of all the instincts, would it not be absurdly pedantic for a critical student of literature to resort to any artificial selection and coordination of his material in order to please the prudes and the pedagogues? And is it not natural to seek that material among the largest literary apparitions of the age?

It is my opinion, then, that the four great authors discussed in the following pages stand, respectively, for the determining strains in a great upsetting movement, and that in the aggregate they bring to view the composite mental and moral impulsion of the times. Through such forceful articulations of current movements the more percipient class of readers have for a long time been

Preface

enabled to foresense, in a manner, the colossal reconstruction of society which needs must follow this monstrous, but presumably final, clash between the irreconcilable elements in the contrasted principles of right and might, the masses and the monarchs.

However, the gathering together of Maeterlinck, Nietzsche, Strindberg, and Tolstoy under the hospitality of a common book-cover permits of a supplementary explanation on the ground of a certain fundamental likeness far stronger than their only too obvious diversities. They are, one and all, radicals in thought, and, with differing strength of intention, reformers of society, inasmuch as their speculations and aspirations are relevant to practical problems of living. And yet what gives them such a durable hold on our attention is not their particular apostolate, but the fact that their artistic impulses ascend from the sublimal regions of the inner life, and that their work somehow brings one into touch with the hidden springs of human action and human fate. This means, in effect, that all of them are mystics by original cast of mind and that notwithstanding any difference, however apparently violent, of views and theories, they follow the same introspec-

Preface

tive path towards the recognition and interpretation of the law of life. From widely separated ethical premises they thus arrive at an essentially uniform appraisal of personal happiness as a function of living.

To those readers who are not disposed to grant the validity of the explanations I have offered, perhaps equality of rank in artistic importance may seem a sufficient criterion for the association of authors, and, apart from all sociologic and philosophic considerations, they may be willing to accept my somewhat arbitrary selection on this single count.

O. H.

April, 1918.

CONTENTS

MAURICE MAETERLINCK

I

THE MYSTICISM OF MAURICE MAETERLINCK

UNDER the terrific atmospheric pressure that has been torturing the civilization of the entire world since the outbreak of the greatest of wars, contemporary literature of the major cast appears to have gone into decline. Even the comparatively few writers recognized as possessing talents of the first magnitude have given way to that pressure and have shrunk to minor size, so that it may be seriously questioned, to say the least, whether during the past forty months or so a single literary work of outstanding and sustained grandeur has been achieved anywhere. That the effect of the universal embattlement upon the art of letters should be, in the main, extremely depressing, is quite natural; but the conspicuous loss of breadth and poise in writers of the first order seems less in accordance with necessity,—at least one might expect a very superior author to rise above that necessity. In any case it is very surprising that it should be a Belgian whose literary personality is almost unique in having remained exempt from the general abridgment of spiritual stature.

It is true that Maurice Maeterlinck, the most eminent literary figure in his sadly stricken country and of unsurpassed standing among the contemporary masters of French letters, has, since the great catastrophe, won no new laurels as a dramatist; and that in the other field cultivated by him, that of the essay, his productiveness has been anything but prolific. But in his case one is inclined to interpret reticence as an eloquent proof of a singularly heroic firmness of character at a time when on both sides of the great divide which now separates the peoples, the cosmopolitan trend of human advance has come to a temporary halt, and the nations have relapsed from their laboriously attained degree of world-citizenship into the homelier, but more immediately virtuous, state of traditional patriotism.

It is a military necessity as well as a birthright of human nature that at a time like the present the patriot is excused from any pharisaical profession of loving his enemy. Before the war, Maeterlinck's writings were animated by humanitarian sympathies of the broadest catholicity. He even had a peculiar affection for the Germans, because doubtless he perceived the existence of a strong kinship between certain essential traits in his spiritual composition and the fundamental tendencies of German philosophy and art. But when Belgium was lawlessly invaded, her ancient towns heinously destroyed, her soil laid waste and drenched with the blood of her people, Maeterlinck, as a son of Belgium, learned to hate the Germans to the utmost of a wise and temperate man's capacity for hatred, and in his war papers collected in *Les Débris de la Guerre*, (1916),[1] which ring with the passionate impulse of the patriot, his outraged sense of justice prevails over the disciplined self-command of the stoic.

He refuses to acquiesce in the lenient discrimination between the guilty Government of Germany and her innocent population: "It is not true that in this gigantic crime there are innocent and guilty, or degrees of guilt. They stand on one level, all those who have taken part in it. . . . It is, very simply, the German, from one end of his country to the other, who stands revealed as a beast of prey which the firm will of our planet finally re-

[1] "The Wrack of the Storm," 1916.

pudiates. We have here no wretched slaves dragged along by a tyrant king who alone is responsible. Nations have the government which they deserve, or rather, the government which they have is truly no more than the magnified and public projection of the private morality and mentality of the nation. . . . No nation can be deceived that does not wish to be deceived; and it is not intelligence that Germany lacks. . . . No nation permits herself to be coerced to the one crime that man cannot pardon. It is of her own accord that she hastens towards it; her chief has no need to persuade, it is she who urges him on." [1]

Such a condemnatory tirade against the despoilers of his fair homeland was normally to be expected from a man of Maeterlinck's depth of feeling. The unexpected thing that happened not long after was that the impulsive promptings of justice and patriotism put themselves into harmony with the guiding principles of his entire moral evolution. The integrity of his philosophy of life, the sterling honesty of his teachings, were thus loyally sealed with the very blood of his heart.— "Before closing this book," he says in the Epi-

[1] "The Wrack of the Storm," pp. 16-18.

Maurice Maeterlinck

logue,[1] "I wish to weigh for the last time in my conscience the words of hatred and malediction which it has made me speak in spite of myself." And then, true prophet that he is, he speaks forth as a voice from the future, admonishing men to prepare for the time when the war is over. What saner advice could at this critical time be given the stay-at-homes than that they should follow the example of the men who return from the trenches? "They detest the enemy," says he, "but they do not hate the man. They recognize in him a brother in misfortune who, like themselves, is submitting to duties and laws which, like themselves, he too believes lofty and necessary." On the other hand, too, not many have sensed as deeply as has Maeterlinck the grandeur to which humanity has risen through the immeasurable pathos of the war. "Setting aside the unpardonable aggression and the inexpiable violation of the treaties, this war, despite its insanity, has come near to being a bloody but magnificent proof of greatness, heroism, and the spirit of sacrifice." And from his profound anguish over the fate of his beloved Belgium this consolation is wrung:

[1] In the English translation this is the chapter preceding the last one and is headed "When the War Is Over," p. 293 ff.; it is separately published in *The Forum* for July, 1916.

Prophets of Dissent

"If it be true, as I believe, that humanity is worth just as much as the sum total of latent heroism which it contains, then we may declare that humanity was never stronger nor more exemplary than now and that it is at this moment reaching one of its highest points and capable of braving everything and hoping everything. And it is for this reason that, despite our present sadness, we are entitled to congratulate ourselves and to rejoice." Altogether, Maeterlinck's thoughts and actions throughout this yet unfinished mighty fate-drama of history challenge the highest respect for the clarity of his intellect and the profoundness of his humanity.

The appalling disaster that has befallen the Belgian people is sure to stamp their national character with indelible marks; so that it is safe to predict that never again will the type of civilization which before the war reigned in the basins of the Meuse and the Scheldt reëstablish itself in its full peculiarity and distinctiveness which was the result of a unique coagency of Germanic and Romanic ingredients of culture. Yet in the amalgam of the two heterogeneous elements a certain competitive antithesis had survived, and manifested itself, in the individual as in the national

Maurice Maeterlinck

life at large, in a number of unreconciled temperamental contrasts, and in the fundamental unlikeness exhibited in the material and the spiritual activities. Witness the contrast between the bustling aggressiveness in the province of practical affairs and the metaphysical drift of modern Flemish art. To any one familiar with the visible materialism of the population in its external mode of living it may have seemed strange to notice how sedulously a numerous set among the younger artists of the land were facing away from their concrete environment, as though to their over-sensitive nervous system it were irremediably offensive. The vigorous solidity of Constantin Meunier, the great plastic interpreter of the "Black Country" of Belgium, found but few wholehearted imitators among the sculptors, while among the painters that robust terrestrialism of which the work of a Rubens or Teniers and their countless disciples was the artistic upshot, was almost totally relinquished, and linear firmness and colorful vitality yielded the day to pallid, discarnately decorative artistry even, in a measure, in the "applied art" products of a Henri van de Velde.

It is in the field of literature, naturally enough, that the contrast is resolved and integrated into a characteristic unity. Very recently Professor A. J. Carnoy has definitely pointed out[1] the striking commixture of the realistic and imaginative elements in the work of the Flemish symbolists. "The vision of the Flemings"—quoting from his own *précis* of his paper—"is very concrete, very exact in all details and gives a durable, real, and almost corporeal presence to the creations of the imagination. All these traits are exhibited in the reveries of the Flemish mystics, ancient and modern. One finds them also no less plainly in the poetic work of Belgian writers of the last generation: Maeterlinck, Verhaeren, Rodenbach, Van Lerberghe, Le Roy, Elskamp, etc."

If we take into account this composite attitude of the Flemish mind we shall be less surprised at the remarkable evolution of a poet-philosopher whose creations seem at first blush to bear no resemblance to the outward complexion of his own age; who seems as far removed temperamentally from his locality and time as were his lineal spiritual ancestors: the Dutchman Ruysbroeck, the Scandinavian Swedenborg, the German Novalis, and the American Emerson—and who in the

---

[1] In a paper read by title before the Modern Language Association of America at Yale University, December 29, 1917.

zenith of his career stands forth as an ardent advocate of practical action while at the same time a
firm believer in the transcendental.

Maeterlinck's romantic antipathy towards the
main drift of the age was a phenomenon which at
the dawn of our century could be observed in a
great number of superior intelligences. Those
fugitives from the dun and sordid materialism of
the day were likely to choose between two avenues
of escape, according to their greater or lesser
inner ruggedness. The more aggressive type
would engage in multiform warfare for the reconstruction of life on sounder principles; whereas
the more meditative professed a real or affected
indifference to practical things and eschewed any
participation in the world's struggle for progress.
And of the quiescent rather than the insurgent
variety of the romantic temper Maurice Maeterlinck was the foremost exponent.

The "romantic longing" seems to have come
into the world in the company of the Christian religion with which it shares its partly outspoken,
partly implied repugnance for the battle of life.
Romantic periods occur in the history of civilization whenever a sufficiently influential set of artistically minded persons have persuaded them-

selves that, in quite a literal sense of the colloquial phrase, they "have no use" for the world; a discovery which would still be true were it stated obversely. The romantic world-view, thus fundamentally oriented by world-contempt, entails, at least in theory, the repudiation of all earthly joys—notably the joy of working—and the renouncement of all worldly ambition; it scorns the cooperative, social disposition, invites the soul to a progressive withdrawal into the inner ego, and ends in complete surrender to one sole aspiration: the search of the higher vision, the vision, that is, of things beyond their tangible reality. To such mystical constructions of the inner eye a certain group of German writers who flourished in the beginning of the nineteenth century and were known as the Romantics, darkly groped their way out of the confining realities of their own time. The most modern spell of romanticism, the one through which our own generation was but yesterday passing, measures its difference from any previous romantic era by the difference between earlier states of culture and our own. Life with us is conspicuously more assertive and aggressive in its social than in its individual expressions, which was by no means always so, and unless the ro-

Maurice Maeterlinck

mantic predisposition adapted itself to this important change it could not relate itself at all intimately to our interests. Our study of Maeterlinck should help us, therefore, to discover possibly in the new romantic tendency some practical and vital bearings.

We find that in the new romanticism esthetic and philosophical impulses are inextricably mixed. Hence the new movement is also playing an indispensable rôle in the modern re-foundation of art. For while acting as a wholesome offset to the so-called naturalism, in its firm refusal to limit inner life to the superficial realities, it at the same time combines with naturalism into a complete recoiling, both of the intellect and the emotions, from any commonplace, or pusillanimous, or mechanical practices of artistry. This latter-day romanticism, moreover, notwithstanding its sky-aspiring outstretch, is akin to naturalism in that, after all, it keeps its roots firmly grounded in the earth; that is to say, it seeks for its ulterior sanctions not in realms high beyond the self; rather it looks within for the "blue flower" of contentedness. Already to the romantics of old the mystic road to happiness was not unknown. It is, for instance, pointed by Novalis: "Inward leads the mysterious way. Within us or nowhere lies eternity with its worlds; within us or nowhere are the past and the future." Viewed separately from other elements of romanticism, this passion for retreating within the central ego is commonly referred to as mysticism; it has a strong hold on many among the moderns, and Maurice Maeterlinck to be properly understood has to be understood as the poet *par excellence* of modern mysticism. By virtue of this special office he deals mainly in concepts of the transcendental, which puzzles the ordinary person accustomed to perceive only material and ephemeral realities. Maeterlinck holds that nothing matters that is not eternal and that what keeps us from enjoying the treasures of the universe is the hereditary resignation with which we tarry in the gloomy prison of our senses. "In reality, we live only from soul to soul, and we are gods who do not know each other." [1] It follows from this metaphysical foundation of his art that instead of the grosser terminology suitable to plain realities, Maeterlinck must depend upon a code of subtle messages in order to establish between himself and his audience a line of spiritual communication. This makes it somewhat difficult for people of

[1] Maeterlinck, "On Emerson."

[14]

cruder endowment to appreciate his meaning, a grievance from which in the beginning many of them sought redress in facile scoffing. Obtuse minds are prone to claim a right to fathom the profound meanings of genius with the same ease with which they expect to catch the meaning of a bill of fare or the daily stock market report.

It must be confessed, however, that even those to whom Maeterlinck's sphere of thought is not so utterly sealed, enter it with a sense of mixed perplexity and apprehension. They feel themselves helplessly conducted through a world situated beyond the confines of their normal consciousness, and in this strange world everything that comes to pass appears at first extremely impracticable and unreal. The action seems "wholly dissevered from common sense and ordinary uses;" the figures behave otherwise than humans; the dialogue is "poised on the edge of a precipice of bathos." It is clear that works so far out of the common have to be approached from the poet's own point of view. "Let the reader move his standpoint one inch nearer the popular standpoint," thus we are warned by Mr. G. K. Chesterton, "and his attitude towards the poet will be harsh, hostile, unconquerable mirth." There are some works that can be appreciated for their good story, even if we fail to realize the author's moral attitude, let alone to grasp the deeper content of his work. "But if we take a play by Maeterlinck we shall find that unless we grasp the particular fairy thread of thought the poet rather lazily flings to us, we cannot grasp anything whatever. Except from one extreme poetic point of view, the thing is not a play; it is not a bad play, it is a mass of clotted nonsense. One whole act describes the lovers going to look for a ring in a distant cave when they both know they have dropped it down the well. Seen from some secret window on some special side of the soul's turret, this might convey a sense of faerie futility in our human life. But it is quite obvious that unless it called forth that one kind of sympathy, it would call forth nothing but laughter. In the same play, the husband chases his wife with a drawn sword, the wife remarking at intervals, 'I am not gay.' Now there may really be an idea in this; the idea of human misfortune coming most cruelly upon the opportunism of innocence; that the lonely human heart says, like a child at a party, 'I am not enjoying myself as I thought I should.' But it is plain that unless one thinks of this idea, and of this idea only, the expression is not in the least unsuccessful pathos,—it is very broad and highly successful farce!"

And so the atmosphere of Maeterlinck's plays is impregnated throughout with oppressive mysteries, and until the key of these mysteries is found there is very little meaning to the plays. Moreover, these mysteries, be they never so stern and awe-inspiring, are irresistibly alluring. The reason is, they are our own mysteries that have somehow escaped our grasp, and that we fain would recapture, because there dwells in every human breast a vague assent to the immortal truth of Goethe's assertion: "The thrill of awe is man's best heritage." [1]

The imaginative equipment of Maeterlinck's dramaturgy is rather limited and, on its face value, trite. In particular are his dramatis personae creatures by no means calculated to overawe by some extraordinary weirdness or power. And yet we feel ourselves touched by an elemental dread and by an overwhelming sense of our human impotence in the presence of these figures who, without seeming supernatural, are certainly not of common

[1] *"Das Schaudern ist der Menschheit bestes Teil."*

flesh and blood; they impress us as surpassingly
strange mainly because somehow they are instinct
with a life fundamentally more real than the superficial reality we know. For they are the mediums
and oracles of the fateful powers that stir human
beings into action.

The poet of mysticism, then, delves into the
mystic sources of our deeds, and makes us stand
reverent with him before the unknowable forces
by which we are controlled. Naturally he is
obliged to shape his visions in dim outline. His
aim is to shadow forth that which no naked eye
can see, and it may be said in passing that he attains this aim with a mastery and completeness
incomparably beyond the dubious skill displayed
more recently by the grotesque gropings of the so-
called futurist school. Perhaps one true secret of
the perturbing strangeness of Maeterlinck's figures
lies in the fact that the basic principle of their life,
the one thoroughly vital element in them, if it does
not sound too paradoxical to say so, is the idea of
death. Maeterlinck's mood and temper are fully
in keeping with the religious dogma that life is but
a short dream—with Goethe he believes that "all
things transitory but as symbols are sent," and
apparently concurs in the creed voiced by one of

Maurice Maeterlinck

Arthur Schnitzler's characters,—that death is the only subject in life worthy of being pondered by the serious mind. "From our death onwards," so he puts it somewhere, "the adventure of the universe becomes our own adventure."

It will be useful to have a bit of personal information concerning our author. He started his active career as a barrister; not by any means auspiciously, it seems, for already in his twenty-seventh year he laid the toga aside. Experience had convinced him that in the forum there were no laurels for him to pluck. The specific qualities that make for success at the bar were conspicuously lacking in his make-up. Far from being eloquent, he has at all times been noted for an unparalleled proficiency in the art of self-defensive silence. He shuns banal conversation and the sterile distractions of promiscuous social intercourse, dreads the hubbub of the city, and has an intense dislike for travel, to which he resorts only as a last means of escape from interviewers, reporters, and admirers. Maeterlinck, it is seen, is anything but *multorum vir hominum*. In order to preserve intact his love of humanity, he finds it expedient to live for the most part by himself, away from the throng "whose very plaudits give the heart a pang;" his fame has always been a source of annoyance to him. The only company he covets is that of the contemplative thinkers of bygone days,—the mystics, gnostics, cabalists, neo-Platonists. Swedenborg and Plotinus are perhaps his greatest favorites. That the war has produced a mighty agitation in the habitual calm of the great Belgian poet-philosopher goes without saying. His love of justice no less than his love of his country aroused every red corpuscle in his virile personality to violent resentment against the invader. Since the war broke out, however, he has published nothing besides a number of ringingly eloquent and singularly pathetic articles and appeals,—so that the character portrait derived from the body of his work has not at this time lost its application to his personality.

In cast of mind, Maeterlinck is sombrously meditative, and he has been wise in framing his outer existence so that it would accord with his habitual detachment. The greater part of his time used to be divided between his charming retreat at *Quatre Chemins,* near Grasse, and the grand old abbey of St. Wandrille in Normandy, which he managed to snatch in the very nick of time from the tightening clutch of a manufacturing concern. With the temperament of a hermit, he has been, nevertheless, a keen observer of life, though one preferring to watch the motley spectacle from the aristocratic privacy of his box, sheltered, as it were, from prying curiosity. Well on in middle age, he is still an enthusiastic out-of-doors man,—gardener, naturalist, pedestrian, wheelman, and motorist, and commands an extraordinary amount of special knowledge in a variety of sports and sciences. In "The Double Garden" he discusses the automobile with the authority of an expert watt-man and mechanician. In one of his other books he evinces an extraordinary erudition in all matters pertaining to the higher education of dogs; and his work on "The Life of the Bee" passes him beyond question with high rank among "thirty-third degree" apiculturists.

One of the characteristics that seem to separate his books, especially those of the earlier period, from the literary tendencies of his age, is their surprising inattention to present social struggles. His metaphysical bias makes him dwell almost exclusively, and with great moral and logical consistency, on aspects of life that are slightly considered by the majority of men yet which he regards as ulteriorly of sole importance.

When men like Maeterlinck are encountered in the world of practical affairs, they are bound to impress us as odd, because of this inversion of the ordinary policies of behavior. But before classing them as "cranks," we might well ask ourselves whether their appraisal of the component values of life does not, after all, correspond better to their true relativity than does our own habitual evaluation. With the average social being, the transcendental bearing of a proposition is synonymous with its practical unimportance. But in his essay on "The Invisible Goodness" Maeterlinck quite properly raises the question: "Is visible life alone of consequence, and are we made up only of things that can be grasped and handled like pebbles in the road?"

Throughout his career Maeterlinck reveals himself in the double aspect of poet and philosopher. In the first period his philosophy, as has alre .dy been amply hinted, is characterized chiefly by aversion from the externalities of life, and by that tense introversion of the mind which forms the mystic's main avenue to the goal of knowledge. But if, in order to find the key to his tragedies and

Maurice Maeterlinck

puppet plays, we go to the thirteen essays representing the earlier trend of his philosophy and issued in 1896 under the collective title, "The Treasure of the Humble," we discover easily that his cast of mysticism is very different from that of his philosophic predecessors and teachers in the fourteenth and nineteenth centuries, in particular from the devotional mysticism of the "Admirable" John Ruysbroeck, and Friedrich von Hardenberg-Novalis. Maeterlinck does not strive after the so-called "spiritual espousals," expounded by the "doctor ecstaticus," Ruysbroeck, in his celebrated treatise where Christ is symbolized as the divine groom and Human Nature as the bride glowing with desire for union with God. Maeterlinck feels too modernly to make use of that ancient sensuous imagery. The main thesis of his mystical belief is that there are divine forces dormant in human nature; how to arouse and release them, constitutes the paramount problem of human life. His doctrine is that a life not thus energized by its own latent divineness is, and must remain, humdrum and worthless. It will at once be noticed that such a doctrine harmonizes thoroughly with the romantic aspiration. Both mystic and romantic teach that, in the last resort, the battlefield

of our fate lies not out in the wide world but that
it is enclosed in the inner self, within the unknown
quantity which we designate as our soul. The visible life, according to this modern prophet of mysticism, obeys the invisible; happiness and unhappiness flow exclusively from the inner sources.

Maeterlinck's speculations, despite their medie-
val provenience, have a practical orientation. He
firmly believes that it is within the ability of mankind to raise some of the veils that cover life's central secret. In unison with some other charitable
students of society, he holds to the faith that a
more highly spiritualized era is dawning, and from
the observed indications he prognosticates a wider
awakening of the sleepbound soul of man. And
certainly some of the social manifestations that
appeared with cumulative force during the constructive period before the war were calculated to
justify that faith. The revival of interest in the
metaphysical powers of man which expressed itself almost epidemically through such widely di-
vergent cults as Theosophy and Christian Science,
was indubitable proof of spiritual yearnings in the
broader masses of the people. And it had a practical counterpart in civic tendencies and reforms
that evidenced a great agitation of the social con-

Maurice Maeterlinck

science. And even to-day, when the great majority feel that the universal embroilment has caused civilized man to fall from his laboriously achieved level, this sage in his lofty solitude feels the redeeming spiritual connotation of our great calamity. "Humanity was ready to rise above itself, to surpass all that it had hitherto accomplished. It has surpassed it. . . . Never before had nations been seen that were able as a whole to understand that the happiness of each of those who live in this time of trial is of no consequence compared with the honor of those who live no more or the happiness of those who are not yet alive. We stand on heights that had not been attained before."

But even for those many who find themselves unable to build very large hopes on the spiritual uplift of mankind through disaster, Maeterlinck's philosophy is a wholesome tonic. In the essay on "The Life Profound" in "The Treasure of the Humble," we are told: "Every man must find for himself in the low and unavoidable reality of common life his special possibility of a higher existence." The injunction, trite though it sound, articulates a moral very far from philistine. For it urges the pursuit of the transcendental self through those feelings which another very great idealist, Friedrich Schiller, describes in magnificent metaphor as

> . . . *"der dunklen Gefühle Gewalt,*
> *die im Herzen wunderbar schliefen."*

In the labyrinth of the subliminal consciousness there lurks, however, a great danger for the seeker after the hidden treasures: the paralyzing effect of fatalism upon the normal energies. Maeterlinck was seriously threatened by this danger during his earlier period. How he eventually contrived his liberation from the clutch of fatalism is not made entirely clear by the progress of his thought. At all events, an era of greater intellectual freedom, which ultimately was to create him the undisputed captain of his soul and master of his fate, was soon to arrive for him. It is heralded by another book of essays: "Wisdom and Destiny." But, as has been stated, we may in his case hardly hope to trace the precise route traveled by the mind between the points of departure and arrival.

So closely are the vital convictions in this truthful writer linked with the artistic traits of his work that without some grasp of his metaphysics even the technical peculiarities of his plays cannot be

Maurice Maeterlinck

fully appreciated. To the mystic temper of mind, all life is secretly pregnant with great meaning, so that none of its phenomena can be deemed inconsequential. Thus, while Maeterlinck is a poet greatly preoccupied with spiritual matters yet nothing to him is more wonderful and worthy of attention than the bare facts and processes of living. Real life, just like the theatre which purports to represent it, manipulates a multiform assortment of stage effects, now coarse and obvious and claptrap, now refined and esoteric, to suit the diversified taste and capacity of the patrons. To the cultured esthetic sense the tragical tendency carries more meaning than the catastrophic finale; our author accordingly scorns, and perhaps inordinately, whatsoever may appear as merely adventitious in the action of plays. "What can be told," he exclaims, "by beings who are possessed of a fixed idea and have no time to live because they have to kill off a rival or a mistress?" The internalized action in his plays is all of one piece with the profound philosophical conviction that the inner life alone matters; that consequently the small and unnoticed events are more worthy of attention than the sensational, cataclysmic moments. "Why wait ye," he asks in that wonderful rhapsody on "Silence" [1] "for Heaven to open at the strike of the thunderbolt? Ye should attend upon the blessed hours when it silently opens—and it is incessantly opening."

His purpose, then, is to reveal the working of hidden forces in their intricate and inseparable connection with external events; and in order that the *vie intérieure* might have the right of way, drama in his practice emancipates itself very far from the traditional realistic methods. "Poetry," he maintains, "has no other purpose than to keep open the great roads that lead from the visible to the invisible." To be sure, this definition postulates, rather audaciously, a widespread spiritual susceptibility. But in Maeterlinck's optimistic anthropology no human being is spiritually so deadened as to be forever out of all communication with the things that are divine and infinite. He fully realizes, withal, that for the great mass of men there exists no intellectual approach to the truly significant problems of life. It is rather through our emotional capacity that our spiritual experience brings us into touch with the final verities. Anyway, the poet of mysticism appeals from the *impasse* of pure reasoning to the voice of the

[1] "The Treasure of the Humble."

[28]

Maurice Maeterlinck

inner oracles. But how to detect in the deepest recesses of the soul the echoes of universal life and give outward resonance to their faint reverberations? That is the artistic, and largely technical, side of the problem.

Obvious it is that if the beholder's collaboration in the difficult enterprise is to be secured, his imagination has to be stirred to a super-normal degree. Once a dramatist has succeeded in stimulating the imaginative activity, he can dispense with a mass of descriptive detail. But he must comply with two irremissible technical demands. In the first place, the *"vie intérieure"* calls forth a *dialogue intérieur;* an esoteric language, I would say, contrived predominantly for the "expressional" functions of speech, as differenced from its "impressional" purposes. Under Swedenborg's fanciful theory of "correspondences" the literal meaning of a word is merely a sort of protective husk for its secret spiritual kernel. It is this inner, essential meaning that Maeterlinck's dialogue attempts to set free. By a fairly simple and consistent code of intimations the underlying meaning of the colloquy is laid bare and a basis created for a more fundamental understanding of the dramatic transactions. Maeterlinck going, at first, to undue lengths in this endeavor, exposed the diction of his dramas to much cheap ridicule. The extravagant use of repetition, in particular, made him a mark for facile burlesque. The words of the Queen in *Princesse Maleine: "Mais ne répetez pas toujours ce que l'on dit,"* were sarcastically turned against the poet himself.

As a result of the extreme simplicity of his dialogue, Maeterlinck was reproached with having invented the "monosyllabic theatre," the "theatre without words," and with having perpetrated a surrogate sort of drama, a hybrid between libretto and pantomime.

The fact, however, is, his characters speak a language which, far from being absurd, as it was at first thought to be by many of his readers, is instinct with life and quite true to life—to life, that is, as made articulate in the intense privacy of dreams, or hallucinations, or moments of excessive emotional perturbation.

The other principal requisite for the attainment of the inner dramatic vitalness in drama is a pervasive atmospheric mood, a sustained *Stimmung*. This, in the case of Maeterlinck, is brought about by the combined employment of familiar and original artistic devices.

Maurice Maeterlinck

The grave and melancholy mood that so deeply impregnates the work of Maeterlinck is tinged in the earlier stage, as has been pointed out, with the sombre coloring of fatalism. In the first few books, in particular, there hovers a brooding sense of terror and an undefinable feeling of desolation. Through *Serres Chaudes* ("Hot Houses"), his first published book, (1889), there runs a tenor of weariness, of ideal yearnings overshadowed by the hopelessness of circumstances. Even in this collection of poems, where so much less necessity exists for a unity of mood than in the plays, Maeterlinck's predilection for scenic effects suggestive of weirdness and superstitious fear became apparent in the recurrent choice of sombre scenic motifs: oppressive nocturnal silence,—a stagnant sheet of water,—moonlight filtered through green windows, etc. The diction, too, through the incessant use of terms like *morne, las, pâle, désire, ennui, tiède, indolent, malade,* exhales as it were a lazy resignation. Temporarily, then, the fatalistic strain is uppermost both in the philosophy and the poetry of the rising young author; and to make matters worse, his is the fatalism of pessimistic despair: Fate is forsworn against man. The objective point of life is death. We constantly receive warnings from within, but the voices are not unequivocal and emphatic enough to save us from ourselves.

Probing the abysses of his subliminal self, the mystic may sense, along with the diviner promptings of the heart, the lurking demons that undermine happiness,—"the malignant powers,"—again quoting Schiller—"whom no man's craft can make familiar"—that element in human nature which in truth makes man "his own worst enemy." It is a search which at this stage of his development Maeterlinck, as a mystic, cannot bring himself to relinquish, even though, pessimistically, he anticipates that which he most dreads to find; in this way, fatalism and pessimism act as insuperable barriers against his artistic self-assertion. His fixed frame of mind confines him to the representation of but one elemental instinct, namely, that of fear. The rustic in the German fairy tale who sallied forth to learn how to shudder,—*gruseln*,— would have mastered the art to his complete satisfaction if favored with a performance or two of such plays as "Princess Maleine," "The Intruder," or "The Sightless." Perhaps no other dramatist has ever commanded a similarly well-equipped arsenal of thrills and terrible foreshadowings. The commonest objects are fraught with ominous forebodings: a white gown lying on a *prie-dieu,* a curtain suddenly set swaying by a puff of air, the melancholy soughing of a clump of trees,—the simplest articles of daily use are converted into awful symbols that make us shiver by their whisperings of impending doom.

Nor in the earlier products of Maeterlinck are the cruder practices of melodrama scorned or spared,—the crash and flash of thunder and lightning, the clang of bells and clatter of chains, the livid light and ghastly shadows, the howling hurricane, the ominous croaking of ravens amid nocturnal solitude, trees illumined by the fiery eyes of owls, bats whirring portentously through the gloom,—so many harbingers of dread and death. And the prophetic import of these tokens and their sort is reinforced by repeated assertions from the persons in the action that never before has anything like this been known to occur. To such a fearsome state are we wrought up by all this uncanny apparatus that at the critical moment a well calculated knock at the door is sufficient to make our flesh creep and our hair stand on end.

Thus, the *vie intérieure* would seem to prerequire for its externalization a completely furnished chamber of horrors. And when it is added that the scene of the action is by preference a lonely churchyard or a haunted old mansion, a crypt, a cavern, a silent forest or a solitary tower, it is easy to understand why plays like "Princess Maleine" could be classed by superficial and unfriendly critics with the gruesome ebullitions of that fantastic quasi-literary occupation to which we owe a well known variety of "water-front" drama and, in fiction, the "shilling shocker." Their immeasurably greater psychological refinement could not save them later on from condemnation at the hands of their own maker. And yet they are not without very great artistic merits. Octave Mirbeau, in his habitual enthusiasm for the out-of-the-ordinary, hailed Maeterlinck, on the strength of "Princess Maleine," as the Belgian Shakespeare, evidently because Maeterlinck derived some of his motifs from "Hamlet": mainly the churchyard scene, and Prince Hjalmar's defiance of the queen, as well as his general want of decision. As a matter of fact, Maeterlinck has profoundly studied, not Shakespeare alone, but the minor Elizabethans as well. He has made an admirable translation of "Macbeth." Early in his career he even translated one of John Ford's Plays, " 'Tis Pity

Maurice Maeterlinck

She's a Whore," one of the coarsest works ever written for the stage, but to which he was attracted by the intrinsic human interest that far outweighs its offensiveness. As for any real kinship of Maeterlinck with Shakespeare, the resemblance between the two is slight. They differ philosophically in the fundamental frame of mind, ethically in the outlook upon life, dramaturgically in the value attached to external action, and humanly,—much to the disadvantage of the Belgian,—in their sense of humor. For unfortunately it has to be confessed that this supreme gift of the gods has been very sparingly dispensed to Maeterlinck. Altogether, whether or no he is to be counted among the disciples of Shakespeare, his works show no great dependence on the master. With far better reason might he be called a debtor to Germanic folklore, especially in its fantastic elements.

A German fairy world it is to which we are transported by Maeterlinck's first dramatic attempt, "Princess Maleine," (1889), a play refashioned after Grimm's tale of the Maid Maleen; only that in the play all the principals come to a harrowing end and that in it an esoteric meaning lies concealed underneath the primitive plot. The action, symbolically interpreted, illustrates the fatalist's doctrine that man is nothing but a toy in the hands of dark and dangerous powers. Practical wisdom does not help us to discern the working of these powers until it is too late. Neither can we divine their presence, for the prophetic apprehension of the future resides not in the expert and proficient, but rather in the helpless or decrepit,—the blind, the feeble-minded, and the stricken in years, or again in young children and in dumb animals. Take the scene in "Princess Maleine" where the murderers, having invaded the chamber, lie there in wait, with bated breath. In the corridor outside, people are unconcernedly passing to and fro, while the only creatures who, intuitively, sense the danger, are the little Prince and a dog that keeps anxiously scraping at the door.

In *L'Intruse* ("The Intruder"), (1890), a one-act play on a theme which is collaterally developed later on in *Les Aveugles* ("The Sightless"), and in *L'Intérieur* ("Home"), the arriving disaster that cannot be shut out by bolts or bars announces itself only to the clairvoyant sense of a blind old man. The household gathered around the table is placidly waiting for the doctor. Only the blind grandfather is anxious and heavy-laden because he alone knows that Death is entering the house, he alone can feel his daughter's life withering away under the breath of the King of Terror: the sightless have a keener sensitiveness than the seeing for what is screened from the physical eye.

It would hardly be possible to name within the whole range of dramatic literature another work so thoroughly pervaded with the chilling horror of approaching calamity. The talk at the table is of the most commonplace,—that the door will not shut properly, and they must send for the carpenter to-morrow. But from the mechanism of the environment there comes cumulative and incremental warning that something extraordinary and fatal is about to happen. The wind rises, the trees shiver, the nightingales break off their singing, the fishes in the pond grow restive, the dogs cower in fear,—an unseen Presence walks through the garden. Then the clanging of a scythe is heard. A cold current of air rushes into the room. Nearer and nearer come the steps. The grandfather insists that a stranger has seated himself in the midst of the family. The lamp goes out. The bell strikes midnight. The old man is sure that somebody is rising from the table. Then suddenly the baby whose voice has never been heard starts crying. Through an inner door steps a deaconess silently crossing herself: the mother of the house is dead.

These incidents in themselves are not necessarily miraculous. There are none of them but might be accounted for on perfectly natural grounds. In fact, very plausible explanations do offer themselves for the weirdest things that come to pass. So, especially, it was a real, ordinary mower that chanced to whet his scythe; yet the apparition of the Old Reaper in person could not cause the chilling consternation produced by this trivial circumstance coming as it does as the climax of a succession of commonplace happenings exaggerated and distorted by a fear-haunted imagination. To produce an effect like that upon an audience whose credulity refuses to be put to any undue strain is a victorious proof of prime artistic ability.

Les Aveugles ("The Sightless"), (1891), is pitched in the same psychological key. The atmosphere is surcharged with unearthly apprehension. A dreary twilight—in the midst of a thick forest—on a lonely island; twelve blind people fretting about the absence of their guardian. He is gone to find a way out of the woods—what can have become of him? From moment to moment the deserted, helpless band grows more fearstricken. The slightest sound becomes the carrier of evil forebodings: the rustling of the foliage, the flapping of a bird's wings, the swelling roar of the nearby sea in its dash against the shore. The bell strikes twelve—they wonder is it noon or night? Then questions, eager and calamitous, pass in whispers among them: Has the leader lost his way? Will he never come back? Has the dam burst apart and will they all be swallowed by the ocean? The pathos is greatly heightened by an extremely delicate yet sure individuation of the figures, as when at the mention of Heaven those not sightless from birth raise their countenance to the sky. And where in the meanwhile is the lost leader? He is seated right in their midst, but smitten by death. They learn it at last through the actions of the dog; besides whom—in striking parallel to "Princess Maleine"—the only other creature able to see is a little child. The horror-stricken unfortunates realize that they can never get home, and that they must perish in the woods.

In *Les Sept Princesses* ("The Seven Princesses"), (1891), although it is one of Maeterlinck's minor achievements, some of the qualities that are common to all his work become peculiarly manifest. This is particularly true of the skill shown in conveying the feeling of the story by means of suitable scenic devices. Most of his plays depend to a considerable degree for their dark and heavy nimbus of unreality upon a studied combination of paraphernalia in themselves neither numerous nor far-sought. In fact, the resulting scenic repertory, too, is markedly limited: a weird forest, a deserted castle with marble staircase and dreamy moonlit terrace, a tower with vaulted dungeons, a dismal corridor flanked by impenetrable chambers, a lighted interior viewed from the garden, a landscape bodefully crêped with twilight—the list nearly exhausts his store of "sets."

The works mentioned so far are hardly more than able exercises preparatory for the ampler and more finished products which were to succeed them. Yet they represent signal steps in the evolution of a new dramatic style, designed, as has already been intimated, to give palpable form to emotional data descried in moments anterior not only to articulation but even to consciousness itself; and for this reason, the plane of the dramatic

Maurice Maeterlinck

action lies deep below the surface of life, down in the inner tabernacle where the mystic looks for the hidden destinies. In his style, Maeterlinck had gradually developed an unprecedented capacity for bringing to light the secret agencies of fate. A portion of the instructed public had already learned to listen in his writings for the finer reverberations that swing in the wake of the uttered phrase, to heed the slightest hints and allusions in the text, to overlook no glance or gesture that might betray the mind of the acting characters. It is true that art to be great must be plain, but that does not mean that the sole test of great art is the response of the simple and apathetic.

In Maeterlinck's first masterpiece, *Pélléas et Mélisande,* (1892), the motives again are drawn up from the lower regions of consciousness; once more the plot is born of a gloomy fancy, and the darkling mood hovering over scene and action attests the persistence of fatalism in the poet. The theory of old King Arkel, the spokesman of the author's personal philosophy, is that one should not seek to be active; one should ever wait on the threshold of Fate. Even the younger people in the play are infected by the morbid doctrine of an inevitable necessity for all things that happen to them: "We do not go where we would go. We do not do that which we would do." Perhaps, however, these beliefs are here enounced for the last time with the author's assent or acquiescence.

In artistic merit "Pélléas and Mélisande" marks a nearer approach to mastery, once the integral peculiarities of the form and method have been granted. Despite a noticeable lack of force, directness, and plasticity in the characterization, the *vie intérieure* is most convincingly expressed. In one of the finest scenes of the play we see the principals at night gazing out upon a measureless expanse of water dotted with scattered lights. The atmosphere is permeated with a reticent yearning of love. The two young creatures, gentle, shy, their souls tinged with melancholy, are drawn towards one another by an ineluctable mutual attraction. Yet, though their hearts are filled to overflowing, not a word of affection is uttered. Their love reveals itself to us even as to themselves, without a loud and jarring declaration, through its very speechlessness, as it were. The situation well bears out the *roi sage* in *Alladine et Palomides:* "There is a moment when souls touch one another and know everything without a need of our opening the lips." There are still

Maurice Maeterlinck

other scenes in this play so tense with emotion that words would be intrusive and dissonant. There is that lovely picture of Mélisande at the window; Pélléas cannot reach up to her hand, but is satisfied to feel her loosened hair about his face. It is a question whether even that immortal love duet in "Romeo and Juliet" casts a poetic spell more enchanting than this. At another moment in the drama, we behold the lovers in Maeterlinck's beloved half-light, softly weeping as they stare with speechless rapture into the flames. And not until the final parting does any word of love pass their lips. In another part of the play Goland, Mélisande's aging husband, who suspects his young stepbrother, Pélléas, of loving Mélisande, conducts him to an underground chamber. We are not told why he has brought him there, and why he has led him to the brink of the pitfall from which there mounts a smell of death. If it be a heinous deed he is brooding, why does he pause in its execution? His terrible struggle does not reveal itself through speech, yet it is eloquently expressed in the wildness of his looks, the trembling of his voice, and the sudden anguished outcry: "Pélléas! Pélléas!"

Evidently Maeterlinck completely achieves the

very purpose to which the so-called Futurists think they must sacrifice all traditional conceptions of Art; and achieves it without any brutal stripping and skinning of the poetic subject, without the hideous exhibition of its *disjecta membra,* and above all, without that implied disqualification for the higher artistic mission which alone could induce a man to limit his service to the dishing-up of chunks and collops, "cubic" or amorphous.

In recognition of a certain tendency towards mannerism that lay in his technique, Maeterlinck, in a spirit of self-persiflage, labeled the book of one-act plays which he next published, (1894), *Trois Petits Drames pour Marionettes* ("Three Little Puppet Plays"). They are entitled, several-ly: *Alladine et Palomides, Intérieur,* and *La Mort de Tintagiles.* While in motifs and ma-terials as well as in the principal points of style these playlets present a sort of epitome of his ar-tistic progression up to date, they also display some new and significant qualities. Of the three the first named is most replete with suggestive sym-bolism and at the same time most remindful of the older plays, especially of "Pélléas and Méli-sande." King Ablamore is in character and de-meanor clearly a counterpart of King Arkel. To be sure he makes a temporary stand against the might of Fate, but his resistance is meek and futile, and his wisdom culminates in the same old fatalistic formula: *"Je sais qu'on ne fait pas ce que l'on voudrait faire."*

L'Intérieur ("Home") handles a theme almost identical with that of *L'Intruse:* Life and Death separated only by a thin pane of glass,—the sudden advent of affliction from a cloudless sky. In this little tragedy a family scene, enacted in "dumb show," is watched from the outside. The play is without suspense in the customary use of the term, since after the first whispered conversation between the bringers of the fateful tidings the audience is fully aware of the whole story:—the daughter of the house, for whose return the little group is waiting, has been found dead in the river. The quiescent mood is sustained to the end; no great outburst of lamentation; the curtain drops the instant the news has been conveyed. But the poignancy of the tragic strain is only enhanced by the repression of an exciting climax.

"The Death of Tintagiles" repeats in a still more harrowing form the fearful predicament of a helpless child treated with so much dramatic tension in Maeterlinck's first tragedy. Again, as in "Princess Maleine," the action of this dramolet attains its high point in a scene where murderous treachery is about to spring the trap set for an innocent young prince. Intuitively he senses the approach of death, and in vain beats his little fists against the door that imprisons him. The situation is rendered more piteous even than in the earlier treatment of the motif, because the door which bars his escape also prevents his faithful sister Ygraine from coming to the rescue.

We have observed in all the plays so far a marked simplicity of construction. *Aglavaine et Selysette*, (1896), denotes a still further simplification. Here the scenic apparatus is reduced to the very minimum, and the psychological premises are correspondingly plain. The story presents a "triangular" love entanglement strangely free from the sensual ingredient; two women dream of sharing, in all purity, one lover—and the dream ends for one of them in heroic self-sacrifice brought to secure the happiness of the rival. However, more noteworthy than the structure of the plot is the fact that the philosophic current flowing through it has perceptibly altered its habitual direction. The spiritual tendency is felt to be turning in its course, and even though fatalism still holds the rule, with

slowly relaxing grip, yet a changed ethical outlook is manifest. Also, this play for the first time
proclaims, though in no vociferous manner, the
duty of the individual toward himself, the duty so
emphatically proclaimed by two of Maeterlinck's
greatest teachers, Ralph Waldo Emerson and
Henrik Ibsen.

The inner philosophic conflict was but of short
duration. In 1898 *La Sagesse et La Destinée*
("Wisdom and Destiny") saw the light. The
metaphor might be taken in a meaning higher and
more precise than the customary, for, coming to
this book from those that preceded is indeed like
emerging from some dark and dismal cave into
the warm and cheering light of the sun. "Wisdom
and Destiny" is a collection of essays and aphor-
isms which stands to this second phase of Maeterlinck's dramaturgy in a relation closely analogous
to that existing between "The Treasure of the
Humble" and the works heretofore surveyed.
Without amounting to a wholesale recantation of
the idea that is central in the earlier set of essays,
the message of the newer set is of a very different
kind. The author of "Wisdom and Destiny" has
not changed his view touching the superiority of

Prophets of Dissent

the intuitional function over the intellectual. The significant difference between the old belief and the new consists simply in this: the latent force of life is no longer imagined as an antagonistic agency; rather it is conceived as a benign energy that makes for a serene acceptance of the world that is. Of this turn in the outlook, the philosophic affirmation of life and the consent of the will to subserve the business of living are the salutary concomitants. Wisdom, in expanding, has burst the prison of fatalism and given freedom to vision. The world, beheld in the light of this emancipation, is not to be shunned by the wise man. Let Fortune bring what she will, he can strip his afflictions of their terrors by transmuting them into higher knowledge. Therefore, pain and suffering need not be feared and shirked; they may even be hailed with satisfaction, for, as is paradoxically suggested in *Aglavaine et Selysette,* they help man *"être heureux en devenant plus triste,"*—to be happy in becoming sadder. The poet, who till now had clung to the conviction that there can be no happy fate, that all our destinies are guided by unlucky stars, now on the contrary persuades us to consider how even calamity may be refined in the medium of wisdom in such fash-

Maurice Maeterlinck

ion as to become an asset of life, and warns us against recoiling in spirit from any reverse of our fortunes. He holds that blows and sorrows cannot undo the sage. Fate has no weapons save those we supply, and "wise is he for whom even the evil must feed the pyre of love." In fine, Fate obeys him who dares to command it. After all, then, man has a right to appoint himself the captain of his soul, the master of his fate.

Yet, for all that, the author of "Wisdom and Destiny" should not be regarded as the partizan and apologist of sadness for the sake of wisdom. If sorrow be a rich mine of satisfaction, joy is by far the richer mine. This new outlook becomes more and more optimistic because of the increasing faculty of such a philosophy to extract from the mixed offerings of life a more near-at-hand happiness than sufferings can possibly afford; not perchance that perpetual grinning merriment over the comicality of the passing spectacle which with so many passes for a "sense of humor," but rather a calm and serious realization of what is lastingly beautiful, good, and true. A person's attainment of this beatitude imposes on him the clear duty of helping others to rise to a similar exalted level of existence. And this duty Maeterlinck seeks to discharge by proclaiming in jubilant accents the concrete reality of happiness. *L'Oiseau Bleu* ("The Blue Bird"), above all other works, illustrates the fact that human lives suffer not so much for the lack of happiness as for the want of being clearly conscious of the happiness they possess. It is seen that the seed of optimism in "The Treasure of the Humble" has sprouted and spread out, and at last triumphantly shot forth through the overlaying fatalism. The newly converted, hence all the more thoroughgoing, optimist, believing that counsel and consolation can come only from those who trust in the regenerative power of hope, throws himself into a mental attitude akin to that of the Christian Scientist, and confidently proceeds to cure the ills of human kind by a categorical denial of their existence. Or perhaps it would be more just to say of Maeterlinck's latter-day outlook, the serenity of which even the frightful experience of the present time has failed to destroy, that instead of peremptorily negating evil, he merely denies its supremacy. All about him he perceives in the midst of the worst wrongs and evils many fertile germs of righteousness; vice itself seems to distil its own antitoxin.

Together with Maeterlinck's optimistic strain,

his individualism gains an unexpected emphasis. "Before one exists for others, one must exist for one's self. The egoism of a strong and clear-sighted soul is of a more beneficent effect than all the devotion of a blind and feeble soul." Here we have a promulgation identical in gist with Emerson's unqualified declaration of moral independence when he says: "Whoso would be a man must be a nonconformist. He who would gather immortal palms must not be hindered by the name of goodness, but must explore if it be goodness. Nothing is at last sacred but the integrity of your own mind. No law can be sacred to me but that of my nature." [1]

His attitude of countenancing the positive joys of living causes Maeterlinck in his later career to reverse his former judgment, and to inveigh, much in the manner of Nietzsche, against the "parasitical virtues." "Certain notions about resignation and self-sacrifice sap the finest moral forces of mankind more thoroughly than do great vices and even crimes. The alleged triumphs over the flesh are in most cases only complete defeats of life." When to such rebellious sentiments is joined an explicit warning against the seductions and intimida-

[1] "Self-Reliance."

tions held out by the official religions—their sugar
plums and dog whips, as Maeterlinck puts it—one
can only wonder how his writings escaped as long
as they did the attention of the authorities that
swing the power of imprimatur and anathema.

Maeterlinck may not be classed unreservedly
as a radical individualist. For whereas a philosophy like that of Nietzsche takes no account of the
"much-too-many," who according to that great
fantasist do not interest anybody except the stat-
istician and the devil, Maeterlinck realizes the
supreme importance of the great mass as the or-
dained transmitters of civilization. The gulf between aristocratic subjectivism, devoted single-
mindedly to the ruthless enforcement of self-in-
terest, and, on the other hand, a self-forgetful social enthusiasm, is bridged in Maeterlinck by an
extremely strong instinct for justice and, moreover, by his firm belief—at least for the time being
—that the same strong instinct exists universally
as a specific trait of human nature. By such a
philosophy Justice, then, is discerned not as a
supra-natural function, but as a function of human
nature as distinguished from nature at large. The
restriction is made necessary by our knowledge of
the observable operations of nature. In particular

would the principle of heredity seem to argue against the reign of justice in the administration of human destinies, inasmuch as we find ourselves quite unable to recognize in the apportionment of pleasure and pain anything like a due ratio of merit. And yet Maeterlinck realizes that perhaps nature measures life with a larger standard than the individual's short span of existence, and warns us in his essay on "Justice" not to indulge our self-conceit in a specious emulation of ways that are utterly beyond our comprehension. After all, then, our poet-philosopher succeeds *foro conscientiæ* in reconciling his cult of self with devotion to the common interest. Morality, in that essay, is defined as the co-ordination of personal desire to the task assigned by nature to the race. And is it not true that a contrary, that is, ascetic concept of morality reduces itself to absurdity through its antagonism to that primal human instinct that makes for the continuity of life?

From the compromise effected between two fairly opposite ethical principles, there emerges in the works of this period something akin to a socialistic tendency. It is organically related to the mystical prepossession of the author's manner of thinking. Maeterlinck gratefully acknowledges that by the search-light of science the uppermost layers of darkness have been dispelled; but realizes also that the deep-seated central enigma still remains in darkness: as much as ever are the primordial causes sealed against a glimpse of finite knowledge. We have changed the names, not the problems. Instead of God, Providence, or Fate, we say Nature, Selection, and Heredity. But in reality do we know more concerning Life than did our ancestors?

What, then, questions the persevering pursuer of the final verities, shall we do in order that we may press nearer to Truth? May we not perchance steep our souls in light that flows from another source than science? And what purer light is there to illumine us than the halo surrounding a contented worker performing his task, not under coercion, but from a voluntary, or it may be instinctive, submission to the law of life? If such subordination of self constitutes the basis of rational living, we shall do well to study its workings on a lowlier and less complicated plane than the human; for instance, in the behavior of the creature that is proverbial for its unflagging industry. For this industry is not motivated by

Maurice Maeterlinck

immediate or selfish wants; it springs from instinctive self-dedication to the common cause. Some people expected from *La Vie des Abeilles* ("The Life of the Bee"), (1901), much brand-new information about matters of apiculture. But in spite of his twenty-five years' experience, Maeterlinck had no startling discoveries to convey to his fellow-hivers. His book on bees is not primarily the result of a specialist's investigations but a poetical record of the observations made by a mind at once romantic and philosophical and strongly attracted to the study of this particular form of community life, because by its organization on a miniature scale it spreads before the student of society a synoptic view of human affairs.

Of the great change that had by now taken place in his conception of life, Maeterlinck was fully cognizant, and made no concealment of it. In the essay on "Justice" he says, with reference to his earlier dramas: "The motive of these little plays was the fear of the Unknown by which we are constantly surrounded," and passes on to describe his religious temper as a sort of compound of the Christian idea of God with the antique idea of Fate, immersed in the profound gloom of hopeless mystery. "The Unknown took chiefly the aspect of a power, itself but blindly groping in the dark, yet disposing with inexorable unfeelingness of the fates of men."

Evidently those same plays are passed once more in self-critical review in *Ardiane et Barbe-Bleue* ("Ardiane and Blue-Beard"), (1899), notwithstanding the fact that the author disclaims any philosophic purpose and presents his work as a mere libretto. We cannot regard it as purely accidental that of Blue-Beard's terror-stricken wives, four,—Selysette, Mélisande, Ygraine, Alladine,—bear the names of earlier heroines, and, besides, that each of these retains with the name also the character of her namesake. The symbolism is too transparent. The child-wives of the cruel knight, forever in a state of trembling fear, are too passive to extricate themselves from their fate, whereas Ardiane succeeds instantly in breaking her captivity, because she has the spirit and strength to shatter the window and let in the light and air. The contrast between her resolute personality and those five inert bundles of misery undoubtedly connotes the difference between the author's paralyzing fatalism in the past and his present dynamic optimism.

Maurice Maeterlinck

A like contrast between dejection and resilience would be brought to light by a comparison of the twelve lyric poems, *Douze Chansons,* (1897), with the *Serres Chaudes.* The mood is still greatly subdued; the new poetry is by no means free from sadness and a strain of resignation. But the half-stifled despair that cries out from the older book returns no dissonant echo in the new.

Even his dramatic technique comes under the sway of Maeterlinck's altered view of the world. The far freer use of exciting and eventful action testifies to increased elasticity and force. This is a marked feature of *Sœur Beatrice* ("Sister Beatrice"), (1900), a miracle play founded on the old story about the recreant nun who, broken from sin and misery, returns to the cloister and finds that during the many years of her absence her part and person have been carried out by the Holy Virgin herself.

Equally, the three other dramas of this epoch— *Aglavaine et Selysette, Monna Vanna,* and *Joyzelle*—are highly available for scenic enactment. Of the three, *Monna Vanna,* (1902), in particular is conspicuous for a wholly unexpected aptitude of characterization, and for the unsurpassed intensity of its situations, which in this isolated case are not cast in a single mood as in the other plays, but are individually distinct and full of dramatic progress, whereas everywhere else the action moves rather sluggishly.

"Monna Vanna" is one of the most brilliantly actable plays of modern times, despite its improbability. A certain incongruity between the realistic and the romantic aspects in the behavior of the principals is saved from offensiveness by a disposition on the part of the spectator to refer it, unhistorically, to the provenience of the story. But as a matter of fact the actors are not fifteenth century Renaissance men and women at all, but mystics, modern mystics at that, both in their reasoning and their morality. It is under a cryptical soul-compulsion that Giovanna goes forth to the unknown condottiere prepared to lay down her honor for the salvation of her people, and that her husband at last conquers his repugnance to her going. Prinzivalle, Guido, Marco, are mystics even to a higher degree than Vanna.

The poignant actualism of "Monna Vanna" lies, however, in the author's frank sympathy with a distinctively modern zest for freedom. The situation between husband and wife is reminiscent of "A Doll's House" in the greedily possessive quality of Guido's affection, with which quality his tyrannous unbelief in Prinzivalle's magnanimity fully accords. But Maeterlinck here goes a step beyond Ibsen. In her married life with Guido, Vanna was meekly contented, "at least as happy as one can be when one has renounced the vague and extravagant dreams which seem beyond human life." When the crisis arrives she realizes that "it is never too late for one who has found a love that can fill a life." Her final rebellion is sanctioned by the author, who unmistakably endorses the venerable Marco's profession of faith that life is always in the right.

"Joyzelle," (1903), inferior to "Monna Vanna" dramaturgically, and in form the most distinctly fantastic of all Maeterlinck's productions, is still farther removed from the fatalistic atmosphere. This play sounds, as the author himself has stated, "the triumph of will and love over destiny or fatality," as against the converse lesson of *Monna Vanna.* The idea is symbolically expressed in the temptations of Lanceor and in the liberation of Joyzelle and her lover from the power of Merlin and his familiar, Arielle, who impersonates the secret forces of the heart.

Aglavaine et Selysette, Monna Vanna, and

Joyzelle mark by still another sign the advent of a new phase in Maeterlinck's evolution; namely, by the characterization of the heroines. Previously, the women in his plays were hardly individualized and none of them can be said to possess a physiognomy strictly her own. Maeterlinck had returned with great partiality again and again to the same type of woman: languid and listless, without stamina and strength, yet at the same time full of deep feeling, and capable of unending devotion—pathetic incorporeal figures feeling their way along without the light of self-consciousness, like some pre-raphaelite species of somnambulists. In the new plays, on the contrary, women of a courageous and venturesome spirit and with a self-possessive assurance are portrayed by preference and with unmistakable approval.

As the technique in the more recent creations of Maeterlinck, so the diction, too, accommodates itself to altered tendencies. Whereas formerly the colloquy was abrupt and fragmentary, it is now couched in cadenced, flowing language, which, nevertheless, preserves the old-time simplicity. The poet himself has criticized his former dialogue. He said it made those figures seem like

deaf people walking in their sleep, whom somebody is endeavoring to arouse from a heavy
dream.

———————

For the limited purpose of this sketch it is not
needful to enter into a detailed discussion of Maeterlinck's latest productions, since such lines as
they add to his philosophical and artistic physiognomy have been traced beforehand. His literary
output for the last dozen years or so is embodied
in six or seven volumes: about two years to a
book seems to be his normal ratio of achievement, the same as was so regularly observed by
Henrik Ibsen, and one that seems rather suitable
for an author whose reserve, dictated by a profound artistic and moral conscience, like his actual performance, calls for admiration and gratitude. During the war he has written, or at least
published, very little. It is fairly safe to assume
that the emotional experience of this harrowing
period will control his future philosophy as its
most potent factor; equally safe is it to predict,
on the strength of his published utterances, that
his comprehensive humanity, that has been put
to such a severe test, will pass unscathed through
the ordeal.

Prophets of Dissent

Of the last group of Maeterlinck's works only two are dramas, namely, "The Blue Bird," (1909), and "Mary Magdalene," (1910). The baffling symbolism of "The Blue Bird" has not stood in the way of a tremendous international stage success; the fact is due much less to the simple line of thought that runs through the puzzle than to the exuberant fancy that gave rise to it and its splendid scenical elaboration. Probably Mr. Henry Rose is right, in his helpful analysis of "The Blue Bird," in venturing the assertion that "by those who are familiar with Swedenborg's teaching 'The Blue Bird' must be recognized as to a very large extent written on lines which are in accordance with what is known as the Science of Correspondences—a very important part of Swedenborg's teachings." But the understanding of this symbolism in its fullness offers very great difficulties. That a definite and consistent meaning underlies all its features will be rather felt than comprehended by the great majority who surely cannot be expected to go to the trouble first of familiarizing themselves with Maeterlinck's alleged code of symbols and then of applying it meticulously to the interpretation of his plays.

Maurice Maeterlinck

"Mary Magdalene," judged from the dramatic point of view, is a quite impressive tragedy, yet a full and sufficient treatment of the very suggestive scriptural legend it is not. The converted courtezan is characterized too abstractly. Instead of presenting herself as a woman consumed with blazing sensuality but in whom the erotic fire is transmuted into religious passion, she affects us like an enacted commentary upon such a most extraordinary experience.

Finally, there are several volumes of essays, to some of which reference has already been made.[1] *Le Temple Enseveli* ("The Buried Temple"), (1902), consists of six disquisitions, all dealing with metaphysical subjects: Justice, The Evolution of Mystery, The Reign of Matter, The Past, Chance, The Future. *Le Double Jardin* ("The Double Garden"), (1904), is much more miscellaneous in its makeup. These are its heterogeneous subjects: The Death of a Little Dog, Monte Carlo, A Ride in a Motor Car, Dueling, The

[1] Considerable liberty has been taken by Maeterlinck in the grouping and naming of his essays upon their republication in the several collections. The confusion caused thereby is greatly increased by the deviation of some of the translated editions from the original volumes as to the sequence of articles, the individual and collective titles, and even the contents themselves.

Prophets of Dissent

Angry Temper of the Bees, Universal Suffrage, The Modern Drama, The Sources of Spring, Death and the Crown (a discussion upon the fatal illness of Edward VII), a View of Rome, Field Flowers, Chrysanthemums, Old-fashioned Flowers, Sincerity, The Portrait of Woman, and Olive Branches (a survey of certain now, alas, obsolete ethical movements of that day). *L'Intelligence des Fleurs* (in the translation it is named "Life and Flowers," in an enlarged issue "The Measure of the Hours," both 1907), takes up, besides the theme of the general caption, the manufacture of perfumes, the various instruments for measuring time, the psychology of accident, social duty, war, prize-fighting, and "King Lear." In 1912, three essays on Emerson, Novalis, and Ruysbroeck appeared collectively, in English, under the title "On Emerson and Other Essays." These originally prefaced certain works of those writers translated by Maeterlinck in his earlier years.

Maeterlinck's most recent publications are *La Mort* (published in English in a considerably extended collection under the title "Our Eternity"), (1913), "The Unknown Guest," (1914), and *Les Débris de la Guerre* ("The Wrack of the

Maurice Maeterlinck

Storm"), (1916).[1] The two first named, having for their central subject Death and the great concomitant problem of the life beyond, show that the author has become greatly interested in psychical research; he even goes so far as to affirm his belief in precognition. In these essays, Theosophy and Spiritism and kindred occult theories are carefully analyzed, yet ingenious as are the author's speculations, they leave anything like a solution of the perplexing riddles far afield. On the whole he inclines to a telepathic explanation of the psychical phenomena, yet thinks they may be due to the strivings of the cosmic intelligence after fresh outlets, and believes that a careful and persistent investigation of these phenomena may open up hitherto undreamt of realms of reality. In general, we find him on many points less assertive than he was in the beginning and inclined to a general retrenchment of the dogmatic element in his philosophic attitude. A significant passage in "The Buried Treasure" teaches us not to deplore the loss of fixed beliefs. "One should never look back with regret to those hours when a great belief abandons us. A faith that becomes extinct,

[1] "The Light Beyond" (1917) is not a new work at all, but merely a combination of parts from "Our Eternity" and "The Wrack of the Storm."

[65]

a means that fails, a dominant idea that no longer dominates us because we think it is our turn to dominate it—these things prove that we are living, that we are progressing, that we are using up a great many things because we are not standing still." Of the gloomy fatalism of his literary beginnings hardly a trace is to be found in the Maeterlinck of to-day. His war-book, "The Wrack of the Storm," breathes a calm optimism in the face of untold disaster. The will of man is put above the power of fate. "Is it possible that fatality—by which I mean what perhaps for a moment was the unacknowledged desire of the planet —shall not regain the upper hand? At the stage which man has reached, I hope and believe so. . . . Everything seems to tell us that man is approaching the day whereon, seizing the most glorious opportunity that has ever presented itself since he acquired a consciousness, he will at last learn that he is able, when he pleases, to control his whole fate in this world." [1] His faith in humanity is built on the heroic virtues displayed in this war. "To-day, not only do we know that these virtues exist: we have taught the world that they are always triumphant, that nothing is lost

[1] "The Wrack of the Storm," p. 144 f.

while faith is left, while honor is intact, while love continues, while the soul does not surrender." . . . Death itself is now threatened with extinction by our heroic race: "The more it exercises its ravages, the more it increases the intensity of that which it cannot touch; the more it pursues its phantom victories, the better does it prove to us that man will end by conquering death."

In the concluding chapter of "Our Eternity," the romantic modification of Maeterlinck's mysticism is made patent in his confession regarding the problem of Knowledge: "I have added nothing to what was already known. I have simply tried to separate what may be true from that which is assuredly not true. . . . Perhaps through our quest for that undiscoverable Truth we shall have accustomed our eyes to pierce the terror of the last hour by looking it full in the face. . . . We need have no hope that any one will utter on this earth the word that shall put an end to our uncertainties. It is very probable, on the contrary, that no one in this world, nor perhaps in the next, will discover the great secret of the universe. And . . . it is most fortunate that it should be so. We have not only to resign ourselves to living in the incomprehensible, but to rejoice that we cannot get out of it. If there were no more insoluble questions . . . infinity would not be infinite; and then we should have forever to curse the fate that placed us in a universe proportionate to our intelligence. The unknown and the unknowable are necessary and will perhaps always be necessary to our happiness. In any case, I would not wish my worst enemy, were his understanding a thousandfold loftier and a thousandfold mightier than mine, to be condemned eternally to inhabit a world of which he had surprised an essential secret. . . ."[1]

So the final word of Maeterlinck's philosophy, after a lifetime of ardent search, clears up none of the tantalizing secrets of our existence. And yet somehow it bears a message that is full of consolation. The value of human life lies in the perpetual movement towards a receding goal. Whoever can identify himself with such a philosophy and accept its great practical lesson, that we shall never reach Knowledge but acquire wisdom in the pursuit, should be able to envisage the veiled countenance of Truth without despair, and even to face with some courage the eternal problem of our being, its reason and its destination.

[1] Quoted from the excellent translation by A. T. de Mattos.

AUGUST STRINDBERG

II

THE ECCENTRICITY OF AUGUST STRINDBERG

ONE cannot speak of August Strindberg with much *gusto*. The most broadminded critic will find himself under necessity to disapprove of him as a man and to condemn so many features of his production that almost one might question his fitness as a subject of literary discussion. Nevertheless, his importance is beyond dispute and quite above the consideration of personal like or dislike, whether we view him in his creative capacity,—as an intellectual and ethical spokesman of his time,—or in his human character,—as a typical case of certain mental and moral maladies which somehow during his time were more or less epidemic throughout the lettered world. We have it on excellent authority that at his début in the literary theatre he made the stage quake with the elemental power of his personality. Gigantic rebels like Ibsen, Bjoernson, Nietzsche, and Tolstoy, we are told, dwindled to normal proportions beside his titanic stature. He aimed to conquer and convert the whole world by his fanatical protest against the rotten civilization of his time. The attempt proved an utter failure. He never could grow into a world-figure, because he lacked the courage as well as the cosmopolitan adaptability needed for intellectual expatriation. Hence, in great contrast to Ibsen, he remained to Europe at large the uncouth Scandinavian, while in the eyes of Scandinavia he was specifically the Swede; and his country-men, even though they acknowledged him their premier poet, treated him, because of his eccentricity, as a national gazing-stock rather than as a genuine national asset. Yet for all that, he ranks as the foremost writer of his country and one of the representative men of the age. His poetic genius is admitted by practically all the critics, while the greatest among them, George Brandes, pronounces him in addition an unsurpassed master in the command of his mother tongue. But his position as a writer is by no means limited to his own little country. For his works have been translated into all civilized languages, and if the circulation of literary products is a safe indication of their influence, then several of Strindberg's books at

August Strindberg

least must be credited with having done something toward shaping the thought of our time upon some of its leading issues. In any case, the large and durable interest shown his productions marks Strindberg as a literary phenomenon of sufficient consequence to deserve some study.

Readers of Strindberg who seek to discover the reason why criticism should have devoted so much attention to an author regarded almost universally with strong disapproval and aversion, will find that reason most probably in the extreme subjectiveness that dominates everything he has written; personal confession, novels, stories, and plays alike share this equality, and even in his historical dramas the figures, despite the minute accuracy of their delineation, are moved by the author's passion, not their own. Rarely, if ever, has a writer of eminence demonstrated a similar incapacity to reproduce the thoughts and feelings of other people. It has been rightly declared that all his leading characters are merely the outward projections of his own sentiments and ideas,—that at bottom he, August Strindberg, is the sole protagonist in all his dramaturgy and fiction.

Strindberg was a man with an omnivorous intellectual curiosity, and he commanded a vast store of knowledge in the fields of history, science, and languages. His "History of the Swedish People" is recognized by competent judges as a very brilliant and scholarly performance. Before he was launched in his literary career, and while still obscurely employed as minor assistant at a library, he earned distinction as a student of the Chinese language, and one product of his research work in that field was even deemed worthy of being read before the *Académie des Inscriptions et Belles Lettres*. In Geology, Chemistry, Botany, he was equally productive. But the taint of eccentricity in his mental fibre prevented his imposing scientific accomplishments from maintaining him in a state of intellectual equilibrium. He laid as much store by things of which he had a mere smattering as by those on which he was an authority, and his resultant unsteadiness caused him to oscillate between opposite scientific enthusiasms even as his self-contradictory personal character involved him in abrupt changes of position, and made him jump from one extreme of behavior to the other.

Strindberg first attracted public notice by the appearance in 1879 of a novel named "The Red Room." Its effect upon a country characterized

August Strindberg

by so keen an observer as George Brandes as perhaps the most conservative in Europe resembled the excitement caused by Schiller's "The Robbers" almost precisely one hundred years before. It stirred up enough dust to change, though not to cleanse, the musty atmosphere of Philistia. For here was instantly recognized the challenge of a radical spirit uprisen in full and ruthless rebellion against each and every time-hallowed usage and tradition. The recollection of that hot-spur agitator bent with every particle of his strength to rouse the world up from its lethargy by his stentorian "J'accuse" and to pass sentence upon it by sheer tremendous vociferation, is almost entirely obliterated to-day by the remembrance of quite another Strindberg:—the erstwhile stormy idealist changed into a leering cynic; a repulsive embodiment of negation, a grimacing Mephistopheles who denies life and light or anything that he cannot comprehend, and to whom the face of the earth appears forever covered with darkness and filth and death and corruption. Indeed this final depictment of August Strindberg, whether or no it be accurately true to life, is a terrible example of what life can make of a man, or a man of his life, if he is neither light enough to be borne by the current of his time, nor strong enough to set his face against the tide and breast it.

The question is, naturally, was Strindberg sincere in the fanatical insurgency of his earlier period, or was his attitude merely a theatrical pose and his social enthusiasm a ranting declamation? In either case, there opens up this other question: Have we reason to doubt the sincerity of the mental changes that were yet to follow,—the genuineness of his pessimism, occultism, and, in the final stage, of his religious conversion? His unexampled hardihood in reversing his opinions and going dead against his convictions could be illustrated in nearly every sphere of thought. At one time a glowing admirer of Rousseau and loudly professing his gospel of nature, he forsook this allegiance, and chose as his new idol Rousseau's very antipode, Voltaire. For many years he was a democrat of the purest water, identified himself with the proletarian cause, and acted as the fiery champion of the poor labor-driven masses against their oppressors; but one fine day, no matter whether it came about directly through his contact with Nietzsche or otherwise, he repudiated socialism, scornfully denouncing it as a tattered remnant of his cast-off Christianity, and arrayed himself

August Strindberg

on the side of the elect, or self-elect, against the "common herd," the "much-too-many." License for the best to govern the rest, became temporarily his battle-cry; and his political ideal suggested nothing less completely absurd than a republic presided over by an oligarchy of autocrats. His unsurpassed reputation as an anti-feminist would hardly prepare us to find his earlier works fairly aglow with sympathy for the woman cause. He held at one time, as did Tolstoy, that art and poetry have a detrimental effect upon the natural character; for which reason the peasant is a more normal being than the lettered man. Especially was he set against the drama, on the ground that it throws the public mind into confusion by its failure to differentiate sharply between the author's own opinions and those of the characters. Literature, he held, should pattern itself after a serious newspaper: it should seek to influence, not entertain. Not only did he drop this pedantic restriction of literature in the end, but in his own practice he had always defied it, because, despite his fierce campaign against art, he could not overcome the force of his artistic impulses. And so in other provinces of thought, too, he reversed his judgment with a temerity and swiftness that greatly offended the feelings and perplexed the intelligence of his followers for the time being and justified the question whether Strindberg had any principles at all. In politics he was by quick turns Anarchist and Socialist, Radical and Conservative, Republican and Aristocrat, Communist and Egoist; in religion, Pietist, Protestant, Deist, Atheist, Occultist, and Roman Catholic. And yet unquestionably he was honest. To blame him merely because he changed his views, and be it never so radically, would be blaming a man for exercising his right to develop. In any man of influence, an unalterable permanency of opinion would be even more objectionable than a frequent shift of his point of view. In recent times the presumable length of a person's intellectual usefulness has been a live subject of discussion which has resulted in some legislation of very questionable wisdom, for instance the setting of an arbitrary age limit for the active service of high-grade teachers. In actual experience men are too old to teach, or through any other function to move the minds of younger people in a forward direction, whenever they have lost the ability to change their own mind. Yet at all events, an eminent author's right of self-reversal must not be exercised at random;

he should refrain from the propagation of new opinions that have not ripened within himself. Which is the same as saying that he should stick to his old opinions until he finds himself inwardly compelled to abandon them. But as a matter of fact, a man like Strindberg, propelled by an unbridled imagination, alert with romantic tendencies, nervously overstrung, kept constantly under a strain by his morbidly sensitive temperament,—and whose brain is consequently a seething chaos of conflicting ideas, is never put to the necessity of changing his mind; his mind keeps changing itself.

It must be as difficult for the literary historian to do Strindberg full justice as it was for the great eccentric himself; when in taking stock, as it were, of his mental equipment, during one of his protracted periods of despondency, he summed himself up in the following picturesque simile: "A monstrous conglomeration, changing its forms according to the observer's point of view and possessing no more reality than the rainbow that is visible to the eyes and yet does not exist." His evolution may be tracked, however, in the detailed autobiography in which he undertook, by a rigorous application of Hippolyte Taine's well-known

theory and method, to account for his temperamental peculiarities on the basis of heredity and
the milieu and to describe the gradual transformation of his character through education and the
external pressure of contemporary intellectual
movements. This remarkable work is like a picture book of ideals undermined, hollowed, and
shattered; a perverse compound of cynicism and
passion, it is unspeakably loathsome to the sense
of beauty and yet, in the last artistic reckoning,
not without great beauty of its own. It divides
the story of Strindberg's life into these consecu-
tive parts: The Son of the Servant; The Author;
The Evolution of a Soul; The Confession of a
Fool; Inferno; Legends; The Rupture; Alone.
The very titles signalize the brutal frankness, or,
shall we say, terrible sincerity of a tale that rum-
mages without piety among the most sacred priva-
cies, and drags forth from intimate nooks and cor-
ners sorrow and squalor and shame enough to
have wrecked a dozen average existences. There
is no mistaking or evading the challenge hurled
by this story: See me as I am, stripped of conventional lies and pretensions! Look upon my
naked soul, covered with scars and open sores.
Behold me in my spasms of love and hate, now in

demoniacal transports, now prostrate with anguish! And if you want to know how I came to be what I am, consider my ancestry, my bringing up, my social environment, and be sure also to pocket your own due share of the blame for my destruction!—Certainly Strindberg's autobiography is not to be recommended as a graduation gift for convent-bred young ladies, or as a soothing diversion for convalescents, but if accepted in a proper sense, it will be found absorbing, informative, and even helpful.

Strindberg never forgave his father for having married below his station. He felt that the good blood of the Strindbergs,—respectable merchants and ministers and country gentlemen,—was worsened by the proletarian strain imported into it through a working girl named Eleonore Ulrike Norling, the mother of August Strindberg and his eleven brothers and sisters. During August's childhood the family lived in extremely straitened circumstances. When a dozen people live cooped up in three rooms, some of them are more than likely to have the joy of youth crushed out of them and crowded from the premises. Here was the first evil that darkened Strindberg's life: he simply was cheated out of his childhood.

Prophets of Dissent

School was no happier place for him than home. His inordinate pride, only sharpened by the consciousness of his parents' poverty which bordered on pauperism, threw him into a state of perpetual rebellion against comrades and teachers. And all this time his inner life was tossed hither and thither by a general intellectual and emotional restlessness due to an insatiable craving for knowledge. At fifteen years of age he had reached a full conviction on the irredeemable evilness of life; and concluded, in a moment of religious exaltation, to dedicate his own earthly existence to the vicarious expiation of universal sin through the mortification of the flesh. Then, of a sudden, he became a voracious reader of rationalistic literature, and turned atheist with almost inconceivable dispatch, but soon was forced back by remorse into the pietistic frame of mind,—only to pass through another reaction immediately after. At this time he claims that earthly life is a punishment or a probation; but that it lies in man's power to make it endurable by freeing himself from the social restraints. He has become a convert to the fantastic doctrine of Jean Jacques Rousseau, that man is good by nature but has been depraved by civilization. Now in his earliest twenties, he

embraces communism with all its implications,—
free love, state parenthood, public ownership of
utilities, equal division of the fruits of labor, and
so forth,—as the sole and sure means of salvation
for humanity.

In the "Swiss Stories," subtitled "Utopias in
Reality," [1] Strindberg demonstrated to his own
satisfaction the smooth and practical workings
of that doctrine. It was difficult for him to understand why the major part of the world seemed so
hesitant about adopting so tempting and equitable
a scheme of living. Yet, for his own person, too,
he soon disavowed socialism, because under a
socialistic régime the individual would be liable to
have his ideas put into uniform, and the remotest
threat of interference with his freedom of thought
was something this fanatical apostle of liberty
could not brook.

In the preface to the "Utopias," he had referred to himself as "a convinced socialist, like all
sensible people"; whereas now he writes: "Idealism and Socialism are two maladies born of lazi-
ness." Having thus scientifically diagnosed the
disease and prescribed the one true specific for it,

[1] The stories deal among other things with the harmonious
communal life in Godin's *Phalanstère*. Strindberg wrote two
descriptions of it, one before, the other after visiting the colony.

namely—how simple!—the total abolition of the industries, he resumes the preaching of Rousseauism in its simon-pure form, orders every man to be his maid-of-all-work and jack-of-all-trades, puts the world on a vegetarian diet, and then wonders why the socialists denounce and revile him as a turncoat and an apostate.

The biography throws an especially vivid light on Strindberg's relation to one of the most important factors of socialism, to wit, the question of woman's rights. His position on this issue is merely a phase of that extreme and practically isolated position in regard to woman in general that has more than any other single element determined the feeling of the public towards him and by consequence fixed his place in contemporary literature. That this should be so is hardly unfair, because no other element has entered so deeply into the structure and fibre of his thought and feeling.

Strindberg, as has been stated, was not from the outset, or perchance constitutionally, an antifeminist. In "The Red Room" he preaches equality of the sexes even in marriage. The thesis of the book is that man and woman are not antagonistic phenomena of life, rather they are modifications of the same phenomenon, made for mutual completion; hence, they can only fulfill their natural destiny through close coöperative comradeship. But there were two facts that prevented Strindberg from proceeding farther along this line of thought. One was his incorrigible propensity to contradiction, the other his excessive subjectiveness which kept him busy building up theories on the basis of personal experience. The prodigious feminist movement launched in Scandinavia by Ibsen and Bjoernson was very repugnant to him, because he felt, not without some just reason, that the movement was for a great many people little more than a fad. So long as art and literature are influenced by fashion, so long there will be and should be revolts against the vogue. Moreover, Strindberg felt that the movement was being carried too far. He was prepared to accompany Ibsen some distance on the way of reform, but refused to subscribe to his verdict that the whole blame for our crying social maladjustments rests with the unwillingness of men to allot any rights whatsoever to women.

Strindberg's play, "Sir Bengt's Wife," printed in 1882, but of much earlier origin, is interpreted by Brandes as a symbolical portrayal of feminine life in Scandinavia during the author's early manhood. The leading feminine figure, a creature wholly incapable of understanding or appreciating the nobler traits in man, is nevertheless treated with sympathy, on the whole. She is represented,—like Selma Bratsberg in Ibsen's "The League of Youth," and Nora Helmer, in "A Doll's House,"—as the typical and normal victim of a partial and unfair training. Her faults of judgment and errors of temper are due to the fact so forcefully descanted upon by Selma, that women are not permitted to share the interests and anxieties of their husbands. We are expressly informed by Strindberg that this drama was intended, in the first place, as an attack upon the romantic proclivities of feminine education; in the second, as an illustration of the power of love to subdue the will; in the third, as a defense of the thesis that woman's love is of a higher quality than man's; and lastly, as a vindication of the right of woman to be her own master. Again, in "Married" he answers the query, Shall women vote? distinctly in the affirmative, although here the fixed idea about the congenital discordance between the sexes, and the identification of love with a struggle for supremacy, has already seized hold of him.

To repeat, there was at first nothing absolutely preposterous about Strindberg's position in regard to the woman movement. On the contrary, his view might have been endorsed as a not altogether unwholesome corrective for the ruling fashion of dealing with the issue by the advocacy of extremes. But by force of his supervening personal grievance against the sex, Strindberg's anti-feminism became in the long run the fixed pole about which gravitated his entire system of social and ethical thought. His campaign against feminism, which otherwise could have served a good purpose by curbing wild militancy, was defeated by its own exaggerations. Granting that feminists had gone too far in the denunciation of male brutality and despotism, Strindberg went still farther in the opposite direction, when he deliberately set out to lay bare the character of woman by dissecting some of her most diabolical incarnations. As has already been said, he was utterly incapable of objective thinking, and under the sting of his miseries in love and marriage, dislike of woman turned into hatred and hatred into frenzy. Henceforth, the entire spectacle of life presented itself to his distorted vision as a perpetual state of war between the sexes: on the one side he saw the male, strong of mind and heart, but in the generosity of strength guileless and over-trustful; on the other side, the female, weak of body and intellect, but shrewd enough to exploit her frailness by linking iniquity to impotence and contriving by her treacherous cunning to enslave her natural superior:—it is the story of Samson and Delilah made universal in its application. Love is shown up as the trap in which man is caught to be shorn of his power. The case against woman is classically drawn up in "The Father," one of the strangest and at the same time most powerful tragedies of Strindberg. The principals of the plot stand for the typical character difference between the sexes as Strindberg sees it; the man being kind-hearted, good-natured, and aspiring, whereas the woman, setting an example for all his succeeding portraits of women, is cunning, though unintelligent and coarse-grained, soulless, yet insanely ambitious and covetous of power. In glaring contrast to the situation made so familiar by Ibsen, we here see the man struggling away from the clutches of a woman who declares frankly that she has never looked at a man without feeling conscious of her superiority over him. In this play the man, a person of ideals and real ability, who is none other than Strindberg himself in one of his matrimonial predicaments, fails to extricate himself from the snare, and ends—both literally and figuratively—by being put into the strait-jacket.

Without classing Strindberg as one of the great world dramatists, it would be narrow-minded, after experiencing the gripping effect of some of his plays, to deny them due recognition, for indeed they would be remarkable for their perspicacity and penetration, even if they were devoid of any value besides. They contain the keenest analyses ever made of the vicious side of feminine character, obtained by specializing, as it were, on the more particularly feminine traits of human depravity. Assuredly the procedure is onesided, but the delineation of a single side of life is beyond peradventure a legitimate artistic enterprise as long as it is not palmed upon us as an accurate and complete picture. Unfortunately, Strindberg's abnormal vision falsifies the things he looks at, and, being steeped in his insuperable prejudice, his pictures of life, in spite of the partial veracity they possess, never rise above the level of caricatures.

Prophets of Dissent

He was incompetent to pass judgment upon an individual woman separately; to him all women were alike, and that means, all unmitigatedly bad! To the objection raised by one of the characters in "The Father": "Oh, there are so many kinds of women," the author's mouthpiece makes this clinching answer: "Modern investigation has pronounced that there is only one kind."

The autobiography of Strindberg is largely inspired by his unreasoning hatred of women; the result, in the main, of his three unfortunate ventures into the uncongenial field of matrimony. In its first part, the account of his life is not without some traces of healthy humor, but as the story progresses, his entire philosophy of life becomes more and more aberrant under the increasing pressure of that obsession. He gets beside himself at the mere mention of anything feminine, and blindly hits away, let his bludgeon land where it will; logic, common sense, and common decency go to the floor before his vehement and brutal assault. Every woman is a born liar and traitor. Her sole aim in life is to thrive parasitically upon the revenue of her favors. Since marriage and prostitution cannot provide a living for all, the oversupply now clamor for admission to the work-mart; but they are incompetent and lazy, and inveterate shirkers of responsibility. With triumphant malice he points to the perfidious readiness of woman to perform her tasks by proxy, that is, to delegate them to hired substitutes: her children are tended and taught by governesses and teachers; her garments are made by dressmakers and seamstresses; the duties of her household she unloads on servants,—and from selfish considerations of vanity, comfort, and love of pleasure, she withdraws even from the primary maternal obligation and lets her young be nourished at the breast of a stranger. Strindberg in his rage never stops to think that the deputies in these cases,—cooks and housemaids and nurses and so forth,—themselves belong to the female sex, by which fact the impeachment is in large part invalidated.

The play bearing the satirical title "Comrades" makes a special application of the theory about the pre-established antagonism of the sexes. In a situation similar to that in "The Father," husband and wife are shown in a yet sharper antithesis of character: a man of sterling character and ability foiled by a woman in all respects his inferior, yet imperiously determined to dominate him. At first she seems to succeed in her ambition, and in the same measure as she assumes a more and more mannish demeanor, the husband's behavior grows more and more effeminate. But the contest leads to results opposite to those in "The Father." Here, the man, once he is brought to a full realization of his plight, arouses himself from his apathy, reasserts his manhood, and, in the ensuing fight for supremacy, routs the usurper and comes into his own. The steps by which he passes through revolt from subjection to self-liberation, are cleverly signaled by his outward transformation, as he abandons the womanish style of dressing imposed on him by his wife's whim and indignantly flings into a corner the feminine costume which she would make him wear at the ball.

─────────

Leaving aside, then, all question as to their artistic value, Strindberg's dramas are deserving of attention as experiments in a fairly unexplored field of analytic psychology. They are the first literary creations of any great importance begotten by such bitter hatred of woman. The anti-feminism of Strindberg's predecessors, not excepting that arch-misogynist, Arthur Schopenhauer himself, sprang from contempt, not from abhor-

August Strindberg

rence and abject fear. In Strindberg, misogyny turns into downright gynophobia. To him, woman is not an object of disdain, but the cruel and merciless persecutor of man. In order to disclose the most dangerous traits of the feminine soul, Strindberg dissects it by a method that corresponds closely to Ibsen's astonishing demonstration of masculine viciousness. The wide-spread dislike for Strindberg's dramas is due, in equal parts, to the detestableness of his male characters, and to the optimistic disbelief of the general public in the reality of womanhood as he represents it. Strindberg's portraiture of the sex appears as a monstrous slander, principally because no other painter has ever placed the model into the same disadvantageous light, and the authenticity of his pictures is rendered suspicious by their abnormal family resemblance. He was obsessed with the petrifying vision of a uniform cruel selfishness staring out of every woman's face: countess, courtezan, or kitchen maid, all are cast in the same gorgon mold.

Strindberg's aversion towards women was probably kindled into action, as has already been intimated, by his disgust at the sudden irruption of woman worship into literature; but, as has also been made clear, only the disillusionments and grievances of his private experience hardened that aversion into implacable hatred. At first he simply declined to ally himself with the feminist cult, because the women he knew seemed unworthy of being worshipped,—little vain dolls, frivolous coquettes, and pedants given to domestic tyranny, of such the bulk was made up. Under the maddening spur of his personal misfortunes, his feeling passed from weariness to detestation, from detestation to a bitter mixture of fear and furious hate. He conceived it as his supreme mission and central purpose in life to unmask the demon with the angel's face, to tear the drapings from the idol and expose to view the hideous ogress that feeds on the souls of men. Woman, in Strindberg's works, is a bogy, constructed out of the vilest ingredients that enter into the composition of human nature, with a kind of convulsive life infused by a remnant of great artistic power. And this grewsome fabric of a diseased imagination, like Frankenstein's monster, wreaks vengeance on its maker. His own mordant desire for her is the lash that drives him irresistibly to his destruction.

It requires no profound psychologic insight to divine in this odious chimera the deplorable abor-

tion of a fine ideal. The distortion of truth ema-
nates in Strindberg's work, as it does in any significant satire or caricature, from indignation over
the contrast between a lofty conception and a
disappointing reality. What, after all, can be the
mission of this hard-featured gallery of females,—
peevish, sullen, impudent, grasping, violent, lecher-
ous, malignant, and vindictive,—if it is not to mark
pravity and debasement with a stigma in the name
of a pure and noble womanhood?

It should not be left unmentioned that we owe
to August Strindberg some works of great perfection fairly free from the black obsession and with
a constructive and consistently idealistic tendency:
splendid descriptions of a quaint people and their
habitat, tinged with a fine sense of humor, as in
"The Hemsoe-Dwellers"; charming studies of
landscape and of floral and animal life, in the
"Portraits of Flowers and Animals"; the colossal
work on the Swedish People, once before referred
to, a history conceived and executed in a thoroughly modern scientific spirit; two volumes of "Swedish Fortunes and Adventures"; most of his historic dramas also are of superior order. But
these works lie outside the scope of the more spe-

cific discussion of Strindberg as a mystic and an eccentric to which this sketch is devoted. We may conclude by briefly considering the final phases of Strindberg's checkered intellectual career, and by summing up his general significance for the age.

It will be recalled that during the middle period of his life, (in 1888), Strindberg came into personal touch with Nietzsche. The effect of the latter's sensational philosophy is clearly perceptible in the works of that period, notably in "Tschandala" and "By the Open Sea." Evidently, Nietzsche, at first, was very congenial to him. For both men were extremely aristocratic in their instincts. For a while, Strindberg endorsed unqualifiedly the heterodox ethics of the towering paranoiac. For one thing, that philosophy supplied fresh food and fuel to his burning rage against womankind, and that was enough to bribe him into swallowing, for the time being, the entire substance of Nietzsche's fantastic doctrine. He took the same ground as Nietzsche, that the race had deteriorated in consequence of its sentimentality, namely through the systematic protection of physical and mental inferiority and unchecked procreation of weaklings. He seconded Nietzsche's motion that society should exterminate its parasites, instead of pampering them. Mankind can only be reinvigorated if the strong and healthy are helped to come into their own. The dreams of the pacifists are fatal to the pragmatic virtues and to the virility of the race. The greatest need is an aggressive campaign for the moral and intellectual sanitation of the world. So let the brain rule over the heart,—and so forth in the same strain.

Very soon, however, Strindberg passed out of the sphere of Nietzsche's influence. The alienation was due as much to his general instability as to the disparity between his pessimistic temper and the joyous exaltation of Zarathustra-ism. His striking reversion to orthodoxy was by no means illogical. Between pessimism and faith there exists a relation that is not very far to seek. When a person has forfeited his peace of soul and cannot find grace before his own conscience, he might clutch as a last hope the promise of vicarious redemption. Extending the significance of his own personal experience to everything within his horizon, and erecting a dogmatic system upon this tenuous generalization, Strindberg reached the conviction that the purpose of living is to suffer, a conviction that threw his philosophy well into line with the religious and ethical ideas of the middle age. Yet even at this juncture his cynicism did not desert him, as witness this comment of his: "Religion must be a punishment, because nobody gets religion who does not have a bad conscience." This avowal preceded his saltatory approach to Roman Catholicism.

In the later volumes of his autobiography he minutely describes the successive crises through which he passed in his agonizing search for certitude and salvation before his spirit found rest in the idea of Destiny which formerly to him was synonymous with Fate and now became synonymous with Providence. "Inferno" pictures his existence as a protracted and unbroken nightmare. He turned determinist, then fatalist, then mystic. The most trifling incidents of his daily life were spelt out according to Swedenborg's "Science of Correspondences" and thereby assumed a deep and terrifying significance. In the most trivial events, such as the opening or shutting of a door, or the curve etched by a raindrop on a dusty pane of glass, he perceived intimations from the occult power that directed his life. Into the most ordinary occurrence of the day he read a divine order, or threat, or chastisement. He was tormented by terrible dreams and visions; in the guise of ferocious beasts, his own sins agonized his flesh. And in the midst of all these tortures he studied and practised the occult arts: magic, astrology, necromancy, alchemy; he concocted gold by hermetical science! To all appearances utterly deranged, he was still lucid enough at intervals to carry on chemical, botanical, and physiological experiments of legitimate worth. Then his reason cleared up once again and put a sudden end to an episode which he has described in these words: "To go in quest of God and to find the devil,—that is what happened to me."

He took leave of Swedenborg as he had taken leave of Nietzsche, yet retained much gratitude for him; the great Scandinavian seer had brought him back to God, so he averred, even though the conversion was effected by picturings of horror.

"Legends," the further continuation of his self-history, shows him vividly at his closest contact with the Catholic Church. But the most satisfactory portion of the autobiography from a human point of view, and from a literary point perhaps altogether the best thing Strindberg has done, is the closing book of the series, entitled "Alone." He wrote it at the age of fifty, during a period of comparative tranquillity of mind, and that fact is manifested by the composure and moderation of its style. Now at last his storm-tossed soul seems to have found a haven. He accepts his destiny, and resigns himself to believing, since knowledge is barred.

But even this state of serenity harbored no permanent peace; it signified merely a temporary suspension of those terrific internal combats.

In Strindberg's case, religious conversion is not an edifying, but on the contrary a morbid and saddening spectacle; it is equal to a declaration of complete spiritual bankruptcy. He turns to the church after finding all other pathways to God blocked. His type of Christianity does not hang together with the labors and struggles of his secular life. A break with his past can be denied to no man; least of all to a leader of men. Only, if he has deserted the old road, he should be able to lead in the new; he must have a new message if he sees fit to cancel the old. Strindberg, however, has nothing to offer at the end. He stands before us timorous and shrinking, the accuser of his fellows turned self-accuser, a beggar stretching forth empty, trembling hands imploring forgiveness of his sins and the salvation of his soul through gracious mediation. His moral asseverations are either blank truisms, or intellectual aberrations. Strindberg has added nothing to the stock of human understanding. A preacher, of course, is not in duty bound to generate original thought. Indeed if such were to be exacted, our pulpits would soon be as sparsely peopled as already are the pews. Ministers who are wondering hard why so many people stay away from church might well stop to consider whether the reason is not that a large portion of mankind has already secured, theoretically, a religious or ethical basis of life more or less identical with the one which churches content themselves with offering. The greatest religious teacher of modern times, Leo Tolstoy, was not by any means a bringer of new truths. The true secret of the tremendous power which nevertheless he wielded over the souls of men was that he extended the practical application of what he believed. If, therefore, we look for a lesson in Strindberg's life as recited by himself, we shall not find it in his religious conversion.

———————

Taken in its entirety, his voluminous yet fragmentary life history is one of the most painful human documents on record. One can hardly peruse it without asking: Was Strindberg insane?

Prophets of Dissent

It is a question which he often put to himself when remorse and self-reproach gnawed at his conscience and when he fancied himself scorned and persecuted by all his former friends. "Why are you so hated?" he asks himself in one of his dialogues, and this is his answer: "I could not endure to see mankind suffer, and so I said and wrote: 'Free yourselves, I shall help.' And so I said to the poor: 'Do not let the rich suck your blood.' And to woman: 'Do not let man oppress you.' And to the children: 'Do not obey your parents if they are unjust.' The consequences,—well, they are quite incomprehensible; for of a sudden I had both sides against me, rich and poor, men and women, parents and children; add to that sickness and poverty, disgraceful pauperism, my divorce, lawsuits, exile, loneliness, and now, to top the climax,—do you believe that I am insane?" From his ultra-subjective point of view, the explanation here given of the total collapse of his fortunes is fairly accurate, at least in the essential aspects. Still, many great men have been pursued by a similar conflux of calamities. Overwhelming misfortunes are the surest test of manhood. How high a person bears up his head under the blows of fate is the best gage of his stature.

August Strindberg

But Strindberg, in spite of his colossal physique, was not cast in the heroic mold. The breakdown of his fortunes caused him to turn traitor to himself, to recant and destroy his intellectual past.

Whether he was actually insane is a question for psychiaters to settle; normal he certainly was not. In medical opinion his modes of reacting to the obstructions and difficulties of the daily life were conclusively symptomatic of neurasthenia. Certain obsessive ideas and idiosyncracies of his, closely bordering upon phobia, would seem to indicate grave psychic disorder. His temper and his world-view were indicative of hypochondria: he perceived only the hostile, never the friendly, aspects of events, people, and phenomena. Dejectedly he declares: "There is falseness even in the calm air and the sunshine, and I feel that happiness has no place in my lot."

Destiny had assembled within him all the doubts and pangs of the modern soul, but had neglected to counterpoise them with positive and constructive convictions; so that when his small store of hopes and prospects was exhausted, he broke down from sheer hollowness of heart. He died a recluse, a penitent, and a renegade to all his past ideas and persuasions.

Prophets of Dissent

Evidently, with his large assortment of defects both of character and of intellect, Strindberg could not be classed as one of the great constructive minds of our period. Viewed in his social importance, he will interest future students of morals chiefly as an agitator, a polemist, and in a fashion, too, as a prophet; by his uniquely aggressive veracity, he rendered a measure of valuable service to his time.

But viewed as a creative writer, both of drama and fiction, he has an incontestable claim to our lasting attention. His work shows artistic ability, even though it rarely attains to greatness and is frequently marred by the bizarre qualities of his style. Presumably his will be a permanent place in the history of literature, principally because of the extraordinary subjective animation of his work. And perhaps in times less depressed than ours its gloominess may act as a valuable antidote upon the popular prejudice against being serious. His artistic profession of faith certainly should save him from wholesale condemnation. He says in one of his prefaces: "Some people have accused my tragedy of being too sad, as though one desired a merry tragedy. People clamor for Enjoyment as though Enjoyment consisted in being foolish. I find enjoyment in the powerful and terrible struggles of life; and the capability of experiencing something, of learning something, gives me pleasure."

The keynote to his literary productions is the cry of the agony of being. Every line of his works is written in the shadow of the sorrow of living. In them, all that is most dismal and terrifying and therefore most tragical, becomes articulate. They are propelled by an abysmal pessimism, and because of this fact, since pessimism is one of the mightiest inspiring forces in literature, August Strindberg, its foremost spokesman, deserves to be read and understood.

FRIEDRICH NIETZSCHE

III

THE EXALTATION OF FRIEDRICH NIETZSCHE

IN these embattled times it is perfectly natural to expect from any discourse on Nietzsche's philosophy first of all a statement concerning the relation of that troublesome genius to the origins of the war; and this demand prompts a few candid words on that aspect of the subject at the start.

For more than three years the public has been persistently taught by the press to think of Friedrich Nietzsche mainly as the powerful promoter of a systematic national movement of the German people for the conquest of the world. But there is strong and definite internal evidence in the writings of Nietzsche against the assumption that he intentionally aroused a spirit of war or aimed in any way at the world-wide preponderance of Germany's type of civilization. Nietzsche had a temperamental loathing for everything that is brutal, a loathing which was greatly intensified by his personal contact with the horrors of war while serving as a military nurse in the campaign of 1870. If there were still any one senseless enough to plead the erstwhile popular cause of Pan-Germanism, he would be likely to find more support for his argument in the writings of the de-gallisized Frenchman, Count Joseph Arthur Gobineau, or of the germanized Englishman, Houston Stewart Chamberlain, than in those of the "hermit of Maria-Sils," who does not even suggest, let alone advocate, German world-predominance in a single line of all his writings. To couple Friedrich Nietzsche with Heinrich von Treitschke as the latter's fellow herald of German ascendancy is truly preposterous. Treitschke himself was bitterly and irreconcilably set against the creator of Zarathustra,[1] in whom ever since "Unzeitgemässe Betrachtungen" he had divined "the good European,"—which to the author of the *Deutsche Geschichte* meant the bad Prussian, and by consequence the bad German.

As a consummate individualist and by the same token a cosmopolite to the full, Nietzsche was the last remove from national, or strictly speaking

---

[1] As is convincingly pointed out in a footnote of J. A. Cramb's "Germany and England."

Friedrich Nietzsche

even from racial, jingoism. Even the imputation
of ordinary patriotic sentiments would have been
resented by him as an insult, for such sentiments
were to him a sure symptom of that gregarious
disposition which was so utterly abhorrent to his
feelings. In his German citizenhood he took no
pride whatsoever. On every occasion that offered
he vented in mordant terms his contempt for the
country of his birth, boastfully proclaiming his own
derivation from alien stock. He bemoaned his
fate of having to write for Germans; averring
that people who drank beer and smoked pipes
were hopelessly incapable of understanding him.
Of this extravagance in denouncing his countrymen
the following account by one of his keenest American interpreters gives a fair idea. "No epithet
was too outrageous, no charge was too farfetched,
no manipulation or interpretation of evidence was
too daring to enter into his ferocious indictment.
He accused the Germans of stupidity, supersti-
tiousness, and silliness; of a chronic weakness of
dodging issues, a fatuous 'barn-yard' and 'green-
pasture' contentment, of yielding supinely to the
commands and exactions of a clumsy and unintelligent government; of degrading education to the
low level of mere cramming and examination pass-

ing; of a congenital inability to understand and absorb the culture of other peoples, and particularly the culture of the French; of a boorish bumptiousness, and an ignorant, ostrichlike complacency; of a systematic hostility to men of genius, whether in art, science, or philosophy; of a slavish devotion to the two great European narcotics, alcohol and Christianity; of a profound beeriness, a spiritual dyspepsia, a puerile mysticism, an old-womanish pettiness, and an ineradicable liking for the obscure, evolving, crepuscular, damp, and shrouded." [1] It certainly requires a violent twist of logic to hold this catalogue of invectives responsible for the transformation of a sluggish and indolent bourgeoisie into a "Volk in Waffen" unified by an indomitable and truculent rapacity.

Neither should Nietzsche's general condemnation of mild and tender forbearance—on the ground that it blocks the purpose of nature—be interpreted as a call to universal militancy. By his ruling it is only supermen that are privileged to carry their will through. But undeniably he does teach that the world belongs to the strong. They may grab it at any temporary loss to the

[1] H. L. Mencken, "The Mailed Fist and Its Prophet." *Atlantic Monthly*, November, 1914.

common run of humanity and, if need be, with sanguinary force, since their will is, ulteriorly, identical with the cosmic purpose.

Of course this is preaching war of some sort, but Nietzsche was not in favor of war on ethnic or ethical grounds, like that fanatical militarist, General von Bernhardi, whom the great mass of his countrymen in the time before the war would have bluntly rejected as their spokesman. Anyway, Nietzsche did not mean to encourage Germany to subjugate the rest of the world. He even deprecated her victory in the bloody contest of 1870, because he thought that it had brought on a form of material prosperity of which internal decay and the collapse of intellectual and spiritual ideals were the unfortunate concomitants. At the same time, the universal decreptitude prevented the despiser of his own people from conceiving a decided preference for some other country. He held that all European nations were progressing in the wrong direction,—the deadweight of exaggerated and misshapen materialism dragged them back and down. English life he deemed almost irredeemably clogged by utilitarianism. Even France, the only modern commonwealth credited by Nietzsche with an indigenous culture, was governed by what he stigmatizes as the life philosophy of the shopkeeper. Nietzsche is destitute of national ideals. In fact he never thinks in terms of politics. He aims to be "a good European, not a good German." In his aversion to the extant order of society he never for a moment advocates, like Rousseau or Tolstoy, a breach with civilization. Cataclysmic changes through anarchy, revolution, and war were repugnant to his ideals of culture. For two thousand years the races of Europe had toiled to humanize themselves, school their character, equip their minds, refine their tastes. Could any sane reformer have calmly contemplated the possible engulfment in another Saturnian age of the gains purchased by that enormous expenditure of human labor? According to Nietzsche's conviction, the new dispensation could not be entered in a book of blank pages. A higher civilization could only be reared upon a lower. So it seems that he is quite wrongly accused of having been an "accessory before the deed," in any literal or legal sense, to the stupendous international struggle witnessed to-day. And we may pass on to consider in what other way he was a vital factor of modern social development. For whatever we may think of the political value

Friedrich Nietzsche

of his teachings, it is impossible to deny their arousing and inspiriting effect upon the intellectual, moral, and artistic faculties of his epoch and ours.

It should be clearly understood that the significance of Nietzsche for our age is not to be explained by any weighty discovery in the realm of knowledge. Nietzsche's merit consists not in any unriddling of the universe by a metaphysical key to its secrets, but rather in the diffusion of a new intellectual light elucidating human consciousness in regard to the purpose and the end of existence., Nietzsche has no objective truths to teach, indeed he acknowledges no truth other than subjective. Nor does he put any faith in bare logic, but on the contrary pronounces it one of mankind's greatest misfortunes. His argumentation is not sustained and progressive, but desultory, impressionistic, and freely repetitional; slashing aphorism is its most effective tool. And so, in the sense of the schools, he is not a philosopher at all; quite the contrary, an implacable enemy of the *métier*. And yet the formative and directive influence of his vaticinations, enunciated with tremendous spiritual heat and lofty gesture, has been very great. His conception of life has acted upon the generation as a moral intoxicant of truly incalculable strength.

Withal his published work, amounting to eighteen volumes, though flagrantly irrational, yet does contain a perfectly coherent doctrine. Only, it is a doctrine to whose core mere peripheric groping will never negotiate the approach. Its essence must be caught by flashlike seizure and cannot be conveyed except to minds of more than the average imaginative sensibility. For its central ideas relate to the remotest ultimates, and its dominant prepossession, the *Overman*, is, in the final reckoning, the creature of a Utopian fancy. To be more precise, Nietzsche extorts from the Darwinian theory of selection a set of amazing connotations by means of the simultaneous shift from the biological to the poetic sphere of thought and from the averagely socialized to an uncompromisingly self-centred attitude of mind. This doubly eccentric position is rendered feasible for him by a whole-souled indifference to exact science and an intense contempt for the practical adjustments of life. He is, first and last, an imaginative schemer, whose visions are engendered by inner exuberance; the propelling power of his philosophy being an intense temperamental enthusiasm

Friedrich Nietzsche

at one and the same time lyrically sensitive and dramatically impassioned. It is these qualities of soul that made his utterance ring with the force of a high moral challenge. All the same, he was not any more original in his ethics than in his theory of knowledge. In this field also his receptive mind threw itself wide open to the flow of older influences which it encountered. The religion of personal advantage had had many a prophet before Nietzsche. Among the older writers, Machiavelli was its weightiest champion. In Germany, Nietzsche's immediate predecessor was "Max Stirner," [1] and as regards foreign thinkers, Nietzsche declared as late as 1888 that to no other writer of his own century did he feel himself so closely allied by the ties of congeniality as to Ralph Waldo Emerson.

The most superficial acquaintance with these writers shows that Nietzsche is held responsible for certain revolutionary notions of which he by no means was the originator. Of the connection of his doctrine with the maxims of "The Prince" and of "The Ego and His Own" (*Der Einzige und sein Eigentum*) [2] nothing further need

[1] His real name was Kaspar Schmidt; he lived from 1806-1856.
[2] By Machiavelli and Stirner, respectively.

be said than that to them Nietzsche owes, directly or indirectly, the principle of "non-morality." However, he does not employ the same strictly intellectual methods. They were logicians rather than moralists, and their ruler-man is in the main a construction of cold reasoning, while the ruler-man of Nietzsche is the vision of a genius whose eye looks down a much longer perspective than is accorded to ordinary mortals. That a far greater affinity of temper should have existed between Nietzsche and Emerson than between him and the two classic non-moralists, must bring surprise to the many who have never recognized the Concord Sage as an exponent of unfettered individualism. Yet in fact Emerson goes to such an extreme of individualism that the only thing that has saved his memory from anathema is that he has not many readers in his after-times, and these few do not always venture to understand him. And Emerson, though in a different way from Nietzsche's, was also a rhapsodist. In his poetry, where he articulates his meaning with far greater unrestraint than in his prose, we find without any difficulty full corroboration of his spiritual kinship with Nietzsche. For instance, where may we turn in the works of the latter for a stronger statement

of the case of Power versus Pity than is contained
in "The World Soul"?

> "He serveth the servant,
>   The brave he loves amain,
>   He kills the cripple and the sick,
>   And straight begins again;
>   For gods delight in gods,
>   And thrust the weak aside,—
>   To him who scorns their charities
>   Their arms fly open wide."

From such a world-view what moral could proceed more logically than that of Zarathustra:
"And him whom ye do not teach to fly, teach—
how to fall quicker"?

But after all, the intellectual origin of Nietzsche's ideas matters but little. Wheresoever they
were derived from, he made them strikingly his
own by raising them to the splendid elevation of
his thought. And if nevertheless he has failed to
take high rank and standing among the sages of
the schools, this shortage in his professional pres-
tige is more than counterbalanced by the wide
reach of his influence among the laity. What
might the re-classification, or perchance even the
re-interpretation, of known facts about life have

signified beside Nietzsche's lofty apprehension of the sacredness of life itself? For whatever may be the social menace of his reasoning, his commanding proclamation to an expectant age of the doctrine that Progress means infinite growth towards ideals of perfection has resulted in a singular reanimation of the individual sense of dignity, served as a potent remedy of social dry-rot, and furthered our gradual emergence from the impenetrable darkness of ancestral traditions.

In seeking an adequate explanation of his power over modern minds we readily surmise that his philosophy draws much of its vitality from the system of science that underlies it. And yet while it is true enough that Nietzsche's fundamental thesis is an offshoot of the Darwinian theory, the violent individualism which is the driving principle of his entire philosophy is rather opposed to the general orientation of Darwinism, since that is social. Not to the author of the "Descent of Man" directly is the modern ethical glorification of egoism indebted for its measure of scientific sanction, but to one of his heterodox disciples, namely to the bio-philosopher W. H. Rolph, who in a volume named "Biologic Problems," with the

Friedrich Nietzsche

subtitle, "An Essay in Rational Ethics,"[1] deals definitely with the problem of evolution in its dynamical bearings. The question is raised, Why do the extant types of life ascend toward higher goals, and, on reaching them, progress toward still higher goals, to the end of time? Under the reason as explained by Darwin, should not evolution stop at a definite stage, namely, when the object of the competitive struggle for existence has been fully attained? Self-preservation naturally ceases to act as an incentive to further progress, so soon as the weaker contestants are beaten off the field and the survival of the fittest is abundantly secured. From there on we have to look farther for an adequate causation of the ascent of species. Unless we assume the existence of an absolutistic teleological tendency to perfection, we are logically bound to connect upward development with favorable external conditions. By substituting for the Darwinian "struggle for existence" a new formula: "struggle for surplus," Rolph advances a new fruitful hypothesis. In all creatures the acquisitive cravings exceed the limit of actual necessity. Under Darwin's interpretation of nature,

[1] *Biologische Probleme, zugleich als Versuch einer rationellen Ethik.* Leipzig, 1882.

the struggle between individuals of the same species would give way to pacific equilibrium as soon as the bare subsistence were no longer in question. Yet we know that the struggle is unending. The creature appetites are not appeased by a normal sufficiency; on the contrary, *"l'appetit vient en mangeant"*; the possessive instinct, if not quite insatiable, is at least coextensive with its opportunities for gratification. Whether or not it be true —as Carlyle claims—that, after all, the fundamental question between any two human beings is, "Can I kill thee, or canst thou kill me?"—at any rate in civilized human society the contest is not waged merely for the naked existence, but mainly for life's increments in the form of comforts, pleasures, luxuries, and the accumulation of power and influence; and the excess of acquisition over immediate need goes as a residuum into the structure of civilization. In plain words, then, social progress is pushed on by individual greed and ambition. At this point Rolph rests the case, without entering into the moral implicates of the subject, which would seem to obtrude themselves upon the attention.

Now to a believer in progressive evolution with a strong ethical bent such a theory brings home man's ulterior responsibility for the betterment of life, and therefore acts as a call to his supreme duty of preparing the ground for the arrival of a higher order of beings. The argument seems simple and clinching. Living nature through a long file of species and genera has at last worked up to the *homo sapiens* who as yet does not even approach the perfection of his own type. Is it a legitimate ambition of the race to mark time on the stand which it has reached and to entrench itself impregnably in its present mediocrity? Nietzsche did not shrink from any of the inferential conclusions logically to be drawn from the biologic argument. If growth is in the purpose of nature, then once we have accepted our chief office in life, it becomes our task to pave the way for a higher genus of man. And the only force that makes with directness for that object is the Will to Power. To foreshadow the resultant human type, Nietzsche resurrected from Goethe's vocabulary the convenient word *Übermensch*—"Overman."

_____

Any one regarding existence in the light of a stern and perpetual combat is of necessity driven at last to the alternative between making the best of life and making an end of it; he must either seek lasting deliverance from the evil of living or endeavor to wrest from the world by any means at his command the greatest sum of its gratifications. It is serviceable to describe the two frames of mind respectively as the optimistic and the pessimistic. But it would perhaps be hasty to conclude that the first of these attitudes necessarily betokens the greater strength of character.

Friedrich Nietzsche's philosophy sprang from pessimism, yet issued in an optimism of unheard-of exaltation; carrying, however, to the end its plainly visible birthmarks. He started out as an enthusiastic disciple of Arthur Schopenhauer; unquestionably the adherence was fixed by his own deep-seated contempt for the complacency of the plebs. But he was bound soon to part company with the grandmaster of pessimism, because he discovered the root of the philosophy of renunciation in that same detestable debility of the will which he deemed responsible for the bovine lassitude of the masses; both pessimism and philistinism came from a lack of vitality, and were symptoms of racial degeneracy. But before Nietzsche finally rejected Schopenhauer and gave his shocking counterblast to the undermining action of pes-

simism, he succumbed temporarily to the spell of
another gigantic personality. We are not concerned with Richard Wagner's musical influence
upon Nietzsche, who was himself a musician of no
mean ability; what is to the point here is the
prime principle of Wagner's art theory. The key
to the Wagnerian theory is found, also, in Schopenhauer's philosophy. Wagner starts from the
pessimistic thesis that at the bottom of the well of
life lies nothing but suffering,—hence living is utterly undesirable. In one of his letters to Franz
Liszt he names as the duplex root of his creative
genius the longing for love and the yearning for
death. On another occasion, he confesses his own
emotional nihilism in the following summary of
Tristan und Isolde: "*Sehnsucht, Sehnsucht, un-
stillbares, ewig neu sich gebärendes Verlangen—
Schmachten und Dursten; einzige Erlösung: Tod,
Sterben, Untergehen, — Nichtmehrerwachen.*" [1]
But from the boundless ocean of sorrow there is
a refuge. It was Wagner's fundamental dogma
that through the illusions of art the individual is
enabled to rise above the hopelessness of the realities into a new cosmos replete with supreme satis-

[1] "Longing, longing, unquenchable desire, reproducing itself
forever anew—thirst and drought; sole deliverance: death, dis-
solution, extinction,—and no awaking."

factions. Man's mundane salvation therefore depends upon the ministrations of art and his own artistic sensitiveness. The glorification of genius is a natural corollary of such a belief.

Nietzsche in one of his earliest works examines Wagner's theory and amplifies it by a rather casuistic interpretation of the evolution of art. After raising the question, How did the Greeks contrive to dignify and ennoble their national existence? he points, by way of an illustrative answer, not perchance to the Periclean era, but to a far more primitive epoch of Hellenic culture, when a total oblivion of the actual world and a transport into the realm of imagination was universally possible. He explains the trance as the effect of intoxication,—primarily in the current literal sense of the word. Such was the significance of the cult of Dionysos. "Through singing and dancing," claims Nietzsche, "man manifests himself as member of a higher community. Walking and talking he has unlearned, and is in a fair way to dance up into the air." That this supposititious Dionysiac phase of Hellenic culture was in turn succeeded by more rational stages, in which the impulsive flow of life was curbed and dammed in by operations of the intellect, is not permitted by Nietzsche to invalidate the argument. By his arbitrary reading of ancient history he was, at first, disposed to look to the forthcoming *Universal-Kunstwerk* [1] as the complete expression of a new religious spirit and as the adequate lever of a general uplift of mankind to a state of bliss. But the typical disparity between Wagner and Nietzsche was bound to alienate them. Wagner, despite all appearance to the contrary, is inherently democratic in his convictions,—his earlier political vicissitudes amply confirm this view,—and fastens his hope for the elevation of humanity through art upon the sort of genius in whom latent popular forces might combine to a new summit. Nietzsche on the other hand represents the extreme aristocratic type, both in respect of thought and of sentiment. "I do not wish to be confounded with and mistaken for these preachers of equality," says he. "For within *me* justice saith: men are not equal." His ideal is a hero of coercive personality, dwelling aloft in solitude, despotically bending the gregarious instincts of the common crowd to his own higher purposes by the dominating force of his Will to Might.

The concept of the Overman rests, as has been

[1] Work of all arts.

shown, upon a fairly solid substructure of plausibility, since at the bottom of the author's reasoning lies the notion that mankind is destined to outgrow its current status; the thought of a humanity risen to new and wondrous heights of power over nature is not necessarily unscientific for being supremely imaginative. The Overman, however, cannot be produced ready made, by any instantaneous process; he must be slowly and persistently willed into being, through love of the new ideal which he is to embody: "All great Love," speaketh Zarathustra, "seeketh to create what it loveth. *Myself* I sacrifice into my love, and *my neighbor* as myself, thus runneth the speech of all creators." Only the fixed conjoint purpose of many generations of aspiring men will be able to create the Overman. "Could you create a God?—Then be silent concerning all gods! But ye could very well create Beyond-man. Not yourselves perhaps, my brethren! But ye could create yourselves into fathers and fore-fathers of Beyond-man; and let this be your best creating. But all creators are hard."

Nietzsche's startlingly heterodox code of ethics coheres organically with the Overman hypothesis, and so understood is certain to lose some of its

Friedrich Nietzsche

aspect of absurdity. The racial will, as we have seen, must be taught to aim at the Overman. But the volitional faculty of the generation, according to Nietzsche, is so debilitated as to be utterly inadequate to its office. Hence, advisedly to stimulate and strengthen the enfeebled will power of his fellow men is the most imperative and immediate task of the radical reformer. Once the power of willing, as such, shall have been,—regardless of the worthiness of its object,—brought back to active life, it will be feasible to give the Will to Might a direction towards objects of the highest moral grandeur.

Unfortunately for the race as a whole, the throng is ineligible for partnership in the auspicious scheme of co-operative procreation; which fact necessitates a segregative method of breeding. The Overman can only be evolved by an ancestry of master-men, who must be secured to the race by a rigid application of eugenic standards, particularly in the matter of mating. Of marriage, Nietzsche has this definition: "Marriage, so call I the will of two to create one who is more than they who created him." For the bracing of the weakened will-force of the human breed it is absolutely essential that master-men, the potential progenitors of the superman, be left unhampered to the impulse of "living themselves out" (*sich auszuleben*),—an opportunity of which under the regnant code of morals they are inconsiderately deprived. Since, then, existing dictates and conventions are a serious hindrance to the requisite autonomy of the master-man, their abolishment might be well. Yet on the other hand, it is convenient that the *Vielzuviele,* the "much-too-many," i. e. the despised generality of people, should continue to be governed and controlled by strict rules and regulations, so that the will of the master-folk might the more expeditiously be wrought. Would it not, then, be an efficacious compromise to keep the canon of morality in force for the general run, but suspend it for the special benefit of master-men, prospective or full-fledged? From the history of the race Nietzsche draws a warrant for the distinction. His contention is that masters and slaves have never lived up to a single code of conduct. Have not civilizations risen and fallen according as they were shaped by this or that class of nations? History also teaches what disastrous consequences follow the loss of caste. In the case of the Jewish people, the domineering type or morals gave way to the servile

Friedrich Nietzsche

as a result of the Babylonian captivity. So long as the Jews were strong, they extolled all manifestations of strength and energy. The collapse of their own strength turned them into apologists of the so-called "virtues" of humility, long-suffering, forgiveness,—until, according to the Judæo-Christian code of ethics, being good came to mean being weak. So races may justly be classified into masters and slaves, and history proves that to the strong goes the empire. The ambitions of a nation are a sure criterion of its worth.

"I walk through these folk and keep mine eyes open. They have become *smaller* and are becoming ever smaller. *And the reason of that is their doctrine of happiness and virtue.*

For they are modest even in their virtue; for they are desirous of ease. But with ease only modest virtue is compatible.

True, in their fashion they learn how to stride and to stride forward. That I call their *hobbling*. Thereby they become an offense unto every one who is in a hurry.

And many a one strideth on and in doing so looketh backward, with a stiffened neck. I rejoice to run against the stomachs of such.

Foot and eyes shall not lie, nor reproach each other for lying. But there is much lying among small folk.

Some of them *will,* but most of them *are willed* merely. Some of them are genuine, but most of them are bad actors.

There are unconscious actors among them, and involuntary actors. The genuine are always rare, especially genuine actors.

Here is little of man; therefore women try to make themselves manly. For only he who is enough of a man will save the woman in woman.

And this hypocrisy I found to be worst among them, that even those who command feign the virtues of those who serve.

'I serve, thou servest, we serve.' Thus the hypocrisy of the rulers prayeth. And, alas, if the highest lord be merely the highest servant!

Alas! the curiosity of mine eye strayed even unto their hypocrisies, and well I divined all their fly-happiness and their humming round window panes in the sunshine.

So much kindness, so much weakness see I. So much justice and sympathy, so much weakness.

Round, honest, and kind are they towards each other, as grains of sand are round, honest, and kind unto grains of sand.

Modestly to embrace a small happiness—they call 'submission'! And therewith they modestly look sideways after a new small happiness.

At bottom they desire plainly one thing most of all: to be hurt by nobody. Thus they oblige all and do well unto them.

But this is *cowardice;* although it be called 'virtue.'

And if once they speak harshly, these small folk,—I hear therein merely their hoarseness. For every draught of air maketh them hoarse.

Prudent are they; their virtues have prudent fingers. But they are lacking in clenched fists; their fingers know not how to hide themselves behind fists.

For them virtue is what maketh modest and tame. Thereby they have made the wolf a dog and man himself man's best domestic animal.

'We put our chair in the midst'—thus saith their

Friedrich Nietzsche

simpering unto me—'exactly as far from dying gladiators as from happy swine.'
This is mediocrity; although it be called moderation." [1]

The only law acknowledged by him who would be a master is the bidding of his own will. He makes short work of every other law. Whatever clogs the flight of his indomitable ambition must be ruthlessly swept aside. Obviously, the enactment of this law that would render the individual supreme and absolute would strike the death-knell for all established forms and institutions of the social body. But such is quite within Nietzsche's intention. They are noxious agencies, ingeniously devised for the enslavement of the will, and the most pernicious among them is the Christian religion, because of the alleged divine sanction conferred by it upon subserviency. Christianity would thwart the supreme will of nature by curbing that lust for domination which the laws of nature as revealed by science sanction, nay prescribe. Nietzsche's ideas on this subject are loudly and over-loudly voiced in *Der Antichrist* ("The Anti-Christ"), written in September 1888 as the first part of a planned treatise in four instalments, entitled *Der Wille zur Macht. Versuch einer*

---

[1] "Thus Spake Zarathustra," pp. 243-245.

Prophets of Dissent

Umwertung aller Werte. ("The Will to Power. An Attempted Transvaluation of All Values".)

The master-man's will, then, is his only law. That is the essence of *Herrenmoral.* And so the question arises, Whence shall the conscience of the ruler-man derive its distinctions between the Right and the Wrong? The arch-iconoclast brusquely stifles this naïve query beforehand by assuring us that such distinctions in their accepted sense do not exist for personages of that grander stamp. Heedless of the time-hallowed concepts that all men share in common, he enjoins mastermen to take their position uncompromisingly outside the confining area of conventions, in the moral independence that dwells "beyond good and evil." Good and Evil are mere denotations, devoid of any real significance. Right and Wrong are not ideals immutable through the ages, nor even the same at any time in all states of society. They are vague and general notions, varying more or less with the practical exigencies under which they were conceived. What was right for my great-grandfather is not *ipso facto* right for myself. Hence, the older and better established a law, the more inapposite is it apt to be to the living de-

mands. Why should the ruler-man bow down to
outworn statutes or stultify his self-dependent
moral sense before the artificial and stupidly uniform moral relics of the dead past? Good is
whatever conduces to the increase of my power,—
evil is whatever tends to diminish it! Only the
weakling and the hypocrite will disagree.

Unmistakably this is a straightout application of the "pragmatic" criterion of truth. Nietzsche's unconfessed and cautious imitators, who
call themselves pragmatists, are not bold enough
to follow their own logic from the cognitive sphere
to the moral. They stop short of the natural
conclusion to which their own premises lead. Morality is necessarily predicated upon specific notions of truth. So if Truth is an alterable and
shifting concept, must not morality likewise be
variable? The pragmatist might just as well come
out at once into the broad light and frankly say:
"Laws do not interest me in the abstract, or for
the sake of their general beneficence; they interest
me only in so far as they affect me. Therefore I
will make, interpret, and abolish them to suit myself."

To Nietzsche the "quest of truth" is a palpable
evasion. Truth is merely a means for the en-

hancement of my subjective satisfaction. It makes not a whit of difference whether an opinion or a judgment satisfies this or that scholastic definition. I call true and good that which furthers my welfare and intensifies my joy in living; and,— to vindicate my self-gratification as a form, indeed the highest, of "social service,"—the desirable thing is that which matters for the improvement of the human stock and thereby speeds the advent of the Superman. "Oh," exclaims Zarathustra, "that ye would understand my word: Be sure to do whatever ye like,—but first of all be such as *can will!* Be sure to love your neighbor as yourself,—but first of all be such as *love themselves,*— as love themselves with great love, with contempt. Thus speaketh Zarathustra, the ungodly."

By way of throwing some light upon this phase of Nietzsche's moral philosophy, it may be added that ever since 1876 he was an assiduous student of Herbert Spencer, with whose theory of social evolution he was first made acquainted by his friend, Paul Rée, who in two works of his own, "Psychologic Observations," (1875), and "On the Origin of Moral Sentiments," (1877), had elaborated upon the Spencerian theory about the genealogy of morals.

Friedrich Nietzsche

The best known among all of Nietzsche's works, *Also Sprach Zarathustra* ("Thus Spake Zarathustra"), is the Magna Charta of the new moral emancipation. It was composed during a sojourn in southern climes between 1883 and 1885, during the convalescence from a nervous collapse, when after a long and critical depression his spirit was recovering its accustomed resilience. Nietzsche wrote his *magnum opus* in solitude, in the mountains and by the sea. His mind always was at its best in settings of vast proportions, and in this particular work there breathes an exaltation that has scarcely its equal in the world's literature. Style and diction in their supreme elation suit the lofty fervor of the sentiment. From the feelings, as a fact, this great rhapsody flows, and to the feelings it makes its appeal; its extreme fascination must be lost upon those who only know how to "listen to reason." The wondrous plastic beauty of the language, along with the high emotional pitch of its message, render "Zarathustra" a priceless poetic monument; indeed its practical effect in chastening and rejuvenating German literary diction can hardly be overestimated. Its value as a philosophic document is much slighter. It is not even organized on severely logical lines. On

the contrary, the four component parts are but
brilliant variations upon a single generic theme,
each in a different clef, but harmoniously united
by the incremental ecstasy of the movement. The
composition is free from monotony, for down to
each separate aphorism every part of it has its
special lyric nuance. The whole purports to
convey in the form of discourse the prophetic
message of Zarathustra, the hermit sage, an ideal-
ized self-portrayal of the author.

In the first book the tone is calm and temperate. Zarathustra exhorts and instructs his disciples, rails at his adversaries, and discloses his
superiority over them. In the soliloquies and dialogues of the second book he reveals himself more
fully and freely as the Superman. The third book
contains the meditations and rhapsodies of Zarathustra now dwelling wholly apart from men, his
mind solely occupied with thought about the
Eternal Return of the Present. In the fourth book
he is found in the company of a few chosen spirits
whom he seeks to imbue with his perfected doctrine. In this final section of the work the deep
lyric current is already on the ebb; it is largely
supplanted by irony, satire, sarcasm, even buffoon-
ery, all of which are resorted to for the pitiless

Friedrich Nietzsche

excoriation of our type of humanity, deemed decrepit by the Sage. The author's intention to present in a concluding fifth division the dying Zarathustra pronouncing his benedictions upon life in the act of quitting it was not to bear fruit.

"Zarathustra"—Nietzsche's terrific assault upon the fortifications of our social structure—is too easily mistaken by facile cavilers for the ravings of an unsound and desperate mind. To a narrow and superficial reading, it exhibits itself as a wholesale repudiation of all moral responsibility and a maniacal attempt to subvert human civilization for the exclusive benefit of the "glorious blonde brute, rampant with greed for victory and spoil." Yet those who care to look more deeply will detect beneath this chimerical contempt of conventional regulations no want of a highminded philanthropic purpose, provided they have the vision necessary to comprehend a love of man oriented by such extremely distant perspectives. At all events they will discover that in this rebellious propaganda an advancing line of life is firmly traced out. The indolent and thoughtless may indeed be horrified by the appalling dangers of the gospel according to Zarathustra. But in reality there is no great cause for alarm. Society may amply rely upon its agencies, even in these stupendous times of universal war, for protection from any disastrous organic dislocations incited by the teachings of Zarathustra, at least so far as the immediate future is concerned—in which alone society appears to be interested. Moreover, our apprehensions are appeased by the sober reflection that by its plain unfeasibleness the whole super-social scheme of Nietzsche is reduced to colossal absurdity. Its limitless audacity defeats any formulation of its "war aims." For what compels an ambitious imagination to arrest itself at the goal of the superman? Why should it not run on beyond that first terminal? In one of Mr. G. K. Chesterton's labored extravaganzas a grotesque sort of super-overman *in spe* succeeds in going beyond unreason when he contrives this lucid self-definition: "I have gone where God has never dared to go. I am above the silly supermen as they are above mere men. Where I walk in the Heavens, no man has walked before me, and I am alone in a garden." It is enough to make one gasp and then perhaps luckily recall Goethe's consoling thought that under the care of Providence the trees will not grow into the heavens. (*"Es ist dafür gesorgt, dass die Bäume nicht in den Him-*

Friedrich Nietzsche

mel wachsen.") As matter of fact, the ideas promulgated in *Also Sprach Zarathustra* need inspire no fear of their winning the human race from its venerable idols, despite the fact that the pull of natural laws and of elemental appetites seems to be on their side. The only effect to be expected of such a philosophy is that it will act as an antidote for moral inertia which inevitably goes with the flock-instinct and the lazy reliance on the accustomed order of things.

Nietzsche's ethics are not easy to valuate, since none of their standards are derived from the orthodox canon. His being a truly personalized form of morality, his principles are strictly cognate to his temperament. To his professed ideals there attaches a definite theory of society. And since his philosophy is consistent in its sincerity, its message is withheld from the man-in-the-street, deemed unworthy of notice, and delivered only to the *élite* that shall beget the superman. To Nietzsche the good of the greatest number is no valid consideration. The great stupid mass exists only for the sake of an oligarchy by whom it is duly exploited under nature's decree that the strong shall prey upon the weak. Let, then, this favored set further the design of nature by systematically encouraging the elevation of their own type.

———————

We have sought to dispel the fiction about the shaping influence of Nietzsche upon the thought and conduct of his nation, and have accounted for the miscarriage of his ethics by their fantastic impracticability. Yet it has been shown also that he fostered in an unmistakable fashion the class-consciousness of the aristocrat, born or self-appointed. To that extent his influence was certainly malign. Yet doubtless he did perform a service to our age. The specific nature of this service, stated in the fewest words, is that to his great divinatory gift are we indebted for an unprecedented strengthening of our hold upon reality. In order to make this point clear we have to revert once more to Nietzsche's transient intellectual relation to pessimism.

We have seen that the illusionism of Schopenhauer and more particularly of Wagner exerted a strong attraction on his high-strung artistic temperament.

Nevertheless a certain realistic counter-drift to the ultra-romantic tendency of Wagner's theory caused him in the long run to reject the faith in

Friedrich Nietzsche

the power of Art to save man from evil. Almost abruptly, his personal affection for the "Master," to whom in his eventual mental eclipse he still referred tenderly at lucid moments, changed to bitter hostility. Henceforth he classes the glorification of Art as one of the three most despicable attitudes of life: Philistinism, Pietism, and Estheticism, all of which have their origin in *cowardice*, represent three branches of the ignominious road of escape from the terrors of living. In three extended diatribes Nietzsche denounces Wagner as the archetype of modern decadence; the most violent attack of all is delivered against the point of juncture in which Wagner's art gospel and the Christian religion culminate: the promise of redemption through pity. To Nietzsche's way of thinking pity is merely the coward's acknowledgment of his weakness. For only insomuch as a man is devoid of fortitude in bearing his own sufferings is he unable to contemplate with equanimity the sufferings of his fellow creatures. Since religion enjoins compassion with all forms of human misery, we should make war upon religion. And for the reason that Wagner's crowning achievement, his *Parsifal,* is a veritable sublimation of Mercy, there can be no truce between its

creator and the giver of the counsel: "Be hard!"
Perhaps this notorious advice is after all not as
ominous as it sounds. It merely expresses rather
abruptly Nietzsche's confidence in the value of self-
control as a means of discipline. If you have
learned calmly to see others suffer, you are yourself able to endure distress with manful composure. "Therefore I wash the hand which helped
the sufferer; therefore I even wipe my soul." But,
unfortunately, such is the frailty of human nature
that it is only one step from indifference about the
sufferings of others to an inclination to exploit
them or even to inflict pain upon one's neighbors
for the sake of personal gain of one sort or another.

Why so hard? said once the charcoal unto the dia-
mond, are we not near relations?

Why so soft? O my brethren, thus I ask you. Are
ye not my brethren?

Why so soft, so unresisting, and yielding? Why is
there so much disavowal and abnegation in your hearts?
Why is there so little fate in your looks?

And if ye are not willing to be fates, and inexorable,
how could ye conquer with me someday?

And if your hardness would not glance, and cut, and
chip into pieces—how could ye create with me some
day?

For all creators are hard. And it must seem blessedness unto you to press your hand upon millenniums as
upon wax,—

Friedrich Nietzsche

Blessedness to write upon the will of millenniums as upon brass,—harder than brass, nobler than brass. The noblest only is perfectly hard.

This new table, O my brethren, I put over you: Become hard! [1]

The repudiation of Wagner leaves a tremendous void in Nietzsche's soul by depriving his enthusiasm of its foremost concrete object. He loses his faith in idealism. When illusions can bring a man like Wagner to such an odious outlook upon life, they must be obnoxious in themselves; and so, after being subjected to pitiless analysis, they are disowned and turned into ridicule. And now, the pendulum of his zeal having swung from one emotional extreme to the other, the great rhapsodist finds himself temporarily destitute of an adequate theme. However, his fervor does not long remain in abeyance, and soon it is absorbed in a new object. Great as is the move it is logical enough. Since illusions are only a hindrance to the fuller grasp of life which behooves all free spirits, Nietzsche energetically turns from self-deception to its opposite, self-realization. In this new spiritual endeavor he relies far more on intuition than on scientific and metaphysical speculation. From his own stand he is certainly justified

[1] "Thus Spake Zarathustra," p. 399, sec. 29.

[145]

in doing this. Experimentation and ratiocination
at the best are apt to disassociate individual realities from their complex setting and then proceed
to palm them off as illustrations of life, when in
truth they are lifeless, artificially preserved speci-
mens.

> *"Encheiresin naturae nennt's die Chemie,*
> *Spottet ihrer selbst und weiss nicht wie."* [1]

Nietzsche's realism, by contrast, goes to the very
quick of nature, grasps all the gifts of life, and
from the continuous flood of phenomena extracts
a rich, full-flavored essence. It is from a sense of
gratitude for this boon that he becomes an idola-
trous worshiper of experience, *"der grosse Jasa-
ger,"*—the great sayer of Yes,—and the most
stimulating optimist of all ages. To Nietzsche
reality is alive as perhaps never to man before.
He plunges down to the very heart of things, ab-
sorbs their vital qualities and meanings, and having himself learned to draw supreme satisfaction
from the most ordinary facts and events, he makes
the common marvelous to others, which, as was
said by James Russell Lowell, is a true test of

---

[1] Goethe's *Faust*, II, ll. 1940-1. Bayard Taylor translates: *En-
cheiresin naturae,* this Chemistry names, nor knows how herself
she banters and blames!

genius. No wonder that deification of reality becomes the dominant *motif* in his philosophy. But again that onesided aristocratic strain perverts his ethics. To drain the intoxicating cup at the feast of life, such is the divine privilege not of the common run of mortals but only of the elect. They must not let this or that petty and artificial convention, nor yet this or that moral command or prohibition, restrain them from the exercise of that higher sense of living, but must fully abandon themselves to its joys. "Since man came into existence he hath had too little joy. That alone, my brethren, is our original sin." [1] The "much-too-many" are doomed to inanity by their lack of appetite at the banquet of life:

Such folk sit down unto dinner and bring nothing with them, not even a good hunger. And now they backbite: "All is vanity!"
But to eat well and drink well, O my brethren, is, verily, no vain art! Break, break the tables of those who are never joyful! [2]

The Will to Live holds man's one chance of this-worldly bliss, and supersedes any care for the remote felicities of any problematic future state. Yet the Nietzschean cult of life is not to be under-

[1] "Thus Spake Zarathustra," p. 120.
[2] *Ibid.*, p. 296, sec. 13.

stood by any means as a banal devotion to the pleasurable side of life alone. The true disciple finds in every event, be it happy or adverse, exalting or crushing, the factors of supreme spiritual satisfaction: joy and pain are equally implied in experience, the Will to Live encompasses jointly the capacity to enjoy and to suffer. It may even be paradoxically said that since man owes some of his greatest and most beautiful achievements to sorrow, it must be a joy and a blessing to suffer. The unmistakable sign of heroism is *amor fati,* a fierce delight in one's destiny, hold what it may.

Consequently, the precursor of the superman will be possessed, along with his great sensibility to pleasure, of a capacious aptitude for suffering. "Ye would perchance abolish suffering," exclaims Nietzsche, "and we,—it seems that we would rather have it even greater and worse than it has ever been. The discipline of suffering,—tragical suffering,—know ye not that only this discipline has heretofore brought about every elevation of man?" "Spirit is that life which cutteth into life. By one's own pain one's own knowledge increaseth;—knew ye that before? And the happiness of the spirit is this: to be anointed and consecrated by tears as a sacrificial animal;—knew ye that before?" And if, then, the tragical pain inherent in life be no argument against Joyfulness, the zest of living can be obscured by nothing save the fear of total extinction. To the disciple of Nietzsche, by whom every moment of his existence is realized as a priceless gift, the thought of his irrevocable separation from all things is unbearable. "'Was this life?' I shall say to Death. 'Well, then, once more!'" And—to paraphrase Nietzsche's own simile—the insatiable witness of the great tragi-comedy, spectator and participant at once, being loath to leave the theatre, and eager for a repetition of the performance, shouts his endless *encore*, praying fervently that in the constant repetition of the performance not a single detail of the action be omitted. The yearning for the endlessness not of life at large, not of life on any terms, but of *this my life* with its ineffable wealth of rapturous moments, works up the extreme optimism of Nietzsche to its stupendous *a priori* notion of infinity, expressed in the name *die ewige Wiederkehr* ("Eternal Recurrence"). It is a staggeringly imaginative concept, formed apart from any evidential grounds, and yet fortified with a fair amount of logical armament. The

universe is imagined as endless in time, although
its material contents are not equally conceived as
limitless. Since, consequently, there must be a
limit to the possible variety in the arrangement
and sequence of the sum total of data, even as in
the case of a kaleidoscope, the possibility of varie-
gations is not infinite. The particular co-ordination of things in the universe, say at this particular
moment, is bound to recur again and again in the
passing of the eons. But under the nexus of cause
and effect the resurgence of the past from the
ocean of time is not accidental nor is the configura-
tion of things haphazard, as is true in the case of
the kaleidoscope; rather, history, in the most inclusive acceptation of the term, is predestined to
repeat itself; this happens through the perpetual
progressive resurrection of its particles. It is then
to be assumed that any aspect which the world has
ever presented must have existed innumerable mil-
lions of times before, and must recur with eternal
periodicity. That the deterministic strain in this
tremendous *Vorstellung* of a cyclic rhythm throb-
bing in the universe entangles its author's fanatical
belief in evolution in a rather serious self-contra-
diction, does not detract from its spiritual lure,

nor from its wide suggestiveness, however incapable it may be of scientific demonstration.

From unfathomed depths of feeling wells up the pæan of the prophet of the life intense.

> O Mensch! Gib Acht!
> Was spricht die tiefe Mitternacht?
> Ich schlief, ich schlief—,
> Aus tiefem Traum bin ich erwacht:—
> Die Welt ist tief,
> Und tiefer als der Tag gedacht.
> Tief ist ihr Weh—,
> Lust—tiefer noch als Herzeleid:
> Weh spricht: Vergeh!
> Doch alle Lust will Ewigkeit—
> Will tiefe, tiefe Ewigkeit! [1]

A timid heart may indeed recoil from the iron necessity of reliving *ad infinitum* its woeful terrestrial fate. But the prospect can hold no terror for the heroic soul by whose fiat all items of experience have assumed important meanings and

[1] O man! Lose not sight!
What saith the deep midnight?
"I lay in sleep, in sleep;
From deep dream I woke to light.
The world is deep,
And deeper than ever day thought it might.
Deep is its woe,—
And deeper still than woe—delight."
Saith woe: "Pass, go!
Eternity's sought by all delight,—
Eternity deep—by all delight.
"Thus Spake Zarathustra," The Drunken Song, p. 174.—The translation but faintly suggests the poetic appeal of the original.

values. He who has cast in his lot with Destiny in spontaneous submission to all its designs, cannot but revere and cherish his own fate as an integral part of the grand unalterable fatality of things.

———————

If this crude presentment of Friedrich Nietzsche's doctrine has not entirely failed of its purpose, the *leitmotifs* of that doctrine will have been readily referred by the reader to their origin; they can be subsumed under that temperamental category which is more or less accurately defined as the *romantic*. Glorification of violent passion,—quest of innermost mysteries,—boundless expansion of self-consciousness,—visions of a future of transcendent magnificence, and notwithstanding an ardent worship of reality a quixotically impracticable detachment from the concrete basis of civic life,—these outstanding characteristics of the Nietzschean philosophy give unmistakable proof of a central, driving, romantic inspiration: Nietzsche shifts the essence and principle of being to a new center of gravity, by substituting the Future for the Present and relying on the untrammeled expansion of spontaneous forces which upon closer examination are found to be without definite aim or practical goal.

For this reason, critically to animadvert upon Nietzsche as a social reformer would be utterly out of place; he is simply too much of a poet to be taken seriously as a statesman or politician. The weakness of his philosophy before the forum of Logic has been referred to before. Nothing can be easier than to prove the incompatibility of some of his theorems. How, for instance, can the absolute determinism of the belief in Cyclic Recurrence be reconciled with the power vested in superman to deflect by his autonomous will the straight course of history? Or, to touch upon a more practical social aspect of his teaching,—if in the order of nature all men are unequal, how can we ever bring about the right selection of leaders, how indeed can we expect to secure the due ascendancy of character and intellect over the gregarious grossness of the demos?

Again, it is easy enough to controvert Nietzsche almost at any pass by demonstrating his unphilosophic onesidedness. Were Nietzsche not stubbornly onesided, he would surely have conceded— as any sane-minded person must concede in these times of suffering and sacrifice—that charity, self-abnegation, and self-immolation might be viewed, not as conclusive proofs of degeneracy, but on the contrary as signs of growth towards perfection. Besides, philosophers of the *métier* are sure to object to the haziness of Nietzsche's idea of Vitality which in truth is oriented, as is his philosophy in general, less by thought than by sentiment.

Notwithstanding his obvious connection with significant contemporaneous currents, the author of "Zarathustra" is altogether too much *sui generis* to be amenable to any crude and rigid classification. He may plausibly be labelled an anarchist, yet no definition of anarchism will wholly take him in. Anarchism stands for the demolition of the extant social apparatus of restraint. Its battle is for the free determination of personal happiness. Nietzsche's prime concern, contrarily, is with internal self-liberation from the obsessive desire for personal happiness in any accepted connotation of the term; such happiness to him does not constitute the chief object of life.

The cardinal point of Nietzsche's doctrine is missed by those who, arguing retrospectively, expound the gist of his philosophy as an incitation to barbarism. Nothing can be more remote from his intentions than the transformation of society into a horde of ferocious brutes. His impeachment of mercy, notwithstanding an appearance of reckless impiety, is in the last analysis no more and no less than an expedient in the truly romantic pursuit of a new ideal of Love. Compassion, in his opinion, hampers the progress towards forms of living that shall be pregnant with a new and superior type of perfection. And in justice to Nietzsche it should be borne in mind that among the various manifestations of that human failing there is none he scorns so deeply as cowardly and petty commiseration of self. It also deserves to be emphasized that he nowhere endorses selfishness when exercised for small or sordid objects. "I love the brave. But it is not enough to be a swordsman, one must also know against whom to use the sword. And often there is more bravery in one's keeping quiet and going past, in order to spare one's self for a worthier enemy: Ye shall have only enemies who are to be hated, but not enemies who are to be despised." [1] Despotism must justify itself by great and worthy ends. And no man must be permitted to be hard towards others who lacks the strength of being even harder towards himself.

[1] "Thus Spake Zarathustra," p. 304.

Prophets of Dissent

At all events it must serve a better purpose to appraise the practical importance of Nietzsche's speculations than blankly to denounce their immoralism. Nietzsche, it has to be repeated, was not on the whole a creator of new ideas. His extraordinary influence in the recent past is not due to any supreme originality or fertility of mind; it is predominantly due to his eagle-winged imagination. In him the emotional urge of utterance was, accordingly, incomparably more potent than the purely intellectual force of opinion: in fact the texture of his philosophy is woven of sensations rather than of ideas, hence its decidedly ethical trend.

The latent value of Nietzsche's ethics in their application to specific social problems it would be extremely difficult to determine. Their successful application to general world problems, if it were possible, would mean the ruin of the only form of civilization that signifies to us. His philosophy, if swallowed in the whole, poisons; in large potations, intoxicates; but in reasonable doses, strengthens and stimulates. Such danger as it harbors has no relation to grossness. His call to the Joy of Living and Doing is no encouragement of vulgar hedonism, but a challenge to persevering

Friedrich Nietzsche

effort. He urges the supreme importance of vigor of body and mind and force of will. "O my brethren, I consecrate you to be, and show unto you the way unto a new nobility. Ye shall become procreators and breeders and sowers of the future.—Not whence ye come be your honor in future, but whither ye go! Your will, and your foot that longeth to get beyond yourselves, be that your new honor!" [1]

It would be a withering mistake to advocate the translation of Nietzsche's poetic dreams into the prose of reality. Unquestionably his Utopia if it were to be carried into practice would doom to utter extinction the world it is devised to regenerate. But it is generally acknowledged that "prophets have a right to be unreasonable," and so, if we would square ourselves with Friedrich Nietzsche in a spirit of fairness, we ought not to forget that the daring champion of reckless unrestraint is likewise the inspired apostle of action, power, enthusiasm, and aspiration, in fine, a prophet of Vitality and a messenger of Hope.

[1] "Thus Spake Zarathustra," p. 294.

LEO TOLSTOY

IV

THE REVIVALISM OF LEO TOLSTOY

IN the intellectual record of our times it is one of the oddest events that the most impressive preacher who has taken the ear of civilized mankind in this generation raised up his voice in a region which in respect of its political, religious, and economic status was until recently, by fairly common consent, ruled off the map of Europe. The greatest humanitarian of his century sprang up in a land chiefly characterized in the general judgment of the outside world by the reactionism of its government and the stolid ignorance of its populace. A country still teeming with analphabeticians and proverbial for its dense medievalism gave to the world a writer who by the great quality of his art and the lofty spiritualism of his teaching was able not only to obtain a wide hearing throughout all civilized countries, but to become a distinct factor in the moral evolution of the age. The stupefying events that have recently revolutionized the Russian state have given the world an inkling of the secrets of the Slavic type of temperament, so mystifying in its commixture of simplicity and strength on the one hand with grossness and stupidity, and on the other hand with the highest spirituality and idealism. For such people as in these infuriated times still keep up some objective and judicious interest in products of the literary art, the volcanic upheaval in the social life of Russia has probably thrown some of Tolstoy's less palpable figures into a greater plastic relief. Tolstoy's own character, too, has become more tangible in its curious composition. The close analogy between his personal theories and the dominant impulses of his race has now been made patent. We are better able to understand the people of whom he wrote because we have come to know better the people for whom he wrote.

The emphasis of Tolstoy's popular appeal was unquestionably enhanced by certain eccentricities of his doctrine, and still more by his picturesque efforts to conform his mode of life, by way of necessary example, to his professed theory of social elevation. The personality of Tolstoy, like the character of the Russian people, is many-sided, and since its aspects are not marked off by convenient lines of division, but are, rather, commingled in the great and varied mass of his literary achievements, it is not easy to make a definitive forecast of his historic position. Tentatively, however, the current critical estimate may be summed up in this: as a creative writer, in particular of novels and short stories, he stood matchless among the realists, and the verdict pronounced at one time by William Dean Howells when he referred to Tolstoy as "the only living writer of perfect fiction" is not likely to be overruled by posterity. Nor will competent judges gainsay his supreme importance as a critic and moral revivalist of society, even though they may be seriously disposed to question whether his principles of conduct constitute in their aggregate a canon of much practical worth for the needs of the western world. As a philosopher or an original thinker, however, he will hardly maintain the place accorded him by the less discerning among his multitudinous followers, for in his persistent attempt to find a new way of understanding life he must be said to have signally failed. Wisdom in him was hampered by Utopian fancies; his dogmas derive from idiosyncrasies and lead into absurdities. Then, too, most of his tenets are easily traced to their sources: in his vagaries as well as in his noblest and soundest aspirations he was merely continuing work which others had prepared.

An objective survey of Tolstoy's work in realistic fiction, in which he ranked supreme, should start with the admission that he was by no means the first arrival among the Russians in that field. Nicholas Gogol, Fedor Dostoievsky, and Ivan Turgenieff had the priority by a small margin. Of these three powerful novelists, Dostoievsky (1821-1881) has probably had an even stronger influence upon modern letters than has Tolstoy himself. He was one of the earliest writers of romance to show the younger generation how to found fiction upon deeper psychologic knowledge. His greatest proficiency lay, as is apt to be the case with writers of a realistic bent, in dealing with the darkest side of life. The wretched and outcast portion of humanity yielded to his skill its most congenial material. His novels—"Poor Folk," (1846), "Memoirs from a Dead House," (1862), "Raskolnikoff," (1866), "The Idiot," (1868), "The Karamasoffs," (1879)—take the reader into company such as had heretofore not gained open entrance to polite literature: criminals, defectives, paupers, and prostitutes. Yet he did not dwell upon the wretchedness of that submerged section of humanity from any perverse delight in what is hideous or for the satisfaction of readers afflicted with morbid curiosity, but from a compelling sense of pity and brotherly love. His works are an appeal to charity. In them, the imperdible grace of the soul shines through the ugliest outward disguise to win a glance from the habitual indifference of fortune's *enfants gâtés*. Dostoievsky preceded Tolstoy in frankly enlisting his talents in the service of his outcast brethren. With the same ideal of the writer's mission held in steady view, Tolstoy turned his attention from the start, and then more and more as his work advanced, to the pitiable condition of the lower orders of society. It must not be forgotten in this connection that his career was synchronous with the growth of a social revolution which, having reached its full force in these days, is making Russia over for better or for worse, and whose wellsprings Tolstoy helps us to fathom.

For the general grouping of his writings it is convenient to follow Tolstoy's own division of his life. His dreamy poetical childhood was succeeded by three clearly distinct stages: first, a score of years filled up with self-indulgent worldliness; next, a nearly equal length of time devoted to artistic ambition, earnest meditation, and helpful social work; last, by a more gradual transition, the ascetic period, covering a long stretch of years given up to religious illumination and to the strenuous advocacy of the Simple Life.

The remarkable spiritual evolution of this great man was apparently governed far more by inborn tendencies than by the workings of experience. Of Tolstoy in his childhood, youth, middle age, and senescence we gain trustworthy impressions from numerous autobiographical documents, but here we shall have to forego anything more than a passing reference to the essential facts of his career. He was descended from an aristocratic family of German stock but domiciled in Russia since the fourteenth century. The year of his birth was 1828, the same as Ibsen's. In youth he was bashful, eccentric, and amazingly ill-favored. The last-named of these handicaps he outgrew but late in life, still later did he get over his bashfulness, and his eccentricity never left him. His penchant for the infraction of custom nearly

Leo Tolstoy

put a premature stop to his career when in his urchin days he once threw himself from a window in an improvised experiment in aerial navigation. At the age of fourteen he was much taken up with subtle speculations about the most ancient and vexing of human problems: the future life, and the immortality of the soul. Entering the university at fifteen, he devoted himself in the beginning to the study of oriental languages, but later on his interest shifted to the law. At sixteen he was already imbued with the doctrines of Jean Jacques Rousseau that were to play such an important rôle in guiding his conduct. In 1846 he passed out of the university without a degree, carrying away nothing but a lasting regret over his wasted time. He went directly to his ancestral estates, with the idealistic intention to make the most of the opportunity afforded him by the patriarchal relationship that existed in Russia between the landholder and the *adscripti glebae* and to improve the condition of his seven hundred dependents. His efforts, however, were foredoomed to failure, partly through his lack of experience, partly also through a certain want of sincerity or tenacity of purpose. The experiment in social education having abruptly come to its end, the disillusionized reformer threw himself headlong into the diversions and dissipations of the capital city. In his "Confession" he refers to that chapter of his existence as made up wholly of sensuality and worldliness. He was inordinately proud of his noble birth,—at college his inchoate apostleship of the universal brotherhood of man did not shield him from a general dislike on account of his arrogance,—and he cultivated the most exclusive social circles of Moscow. He freely indulged the love of sports that was to cling through life and keep him strong and supple even in very old age. (Up to a short time before his death he still rode horseback and perhaps none of the renunciations exacted by his principles came so hard as that of giving up his favorite pastime of hunting.) But he also fell into the evil ways of gilded youth, soon achieving notoriety as a toper, gambler, and *courreur des femmes*. After a while his brother, who was a person of steadier habits and who had great influence over him, persuaded him to quit his profligate mode of living and to join him at his military post. Under the bracing effect of the change, the young man's moral energies quickly revived. In the wilds of the Caucasus he at once grew freer and cleaner; his deep affection for the half-civilized land endeared him both to the Cossack natives and the Russian soldiers. He entered the army at twenty-three, and from November, 1853, up to the fall of Sebastopol in the summer of 1855, served in the Crimean campaign. He entered the famous fortress in November, 1854, and was among the last of its defenders. The indelible impressions made upon his mind by the heroism of his comrades, the awful scenes and the appalling suffering he had to witness, were responsible then and later for descriptions as harrowing and as stirring as any that the war literature of our own day has produced.

In the Crimea he made his début as a writer. Among the tales of his martial period the most popular and perhaps the most excellent is the one called "The Cossacks." Turgenieff pronounced it the best short story ever written in Russian, and it is surely no undue exaggeration to say of Tolstoy's novelettes in general that in point of technical mastery they are unsurpassed.

Sick at heart over the unending bloodshed in the Caucasus the young officer made his way back to Petrograd, and here, lionized in the salons doubly, for his feats at arms and in letters, he seems to have returned, within more temperate limits, to his former style of living. At any rate, in his own judgment the ensuing three years were utterly wasted. The mental inanity and moral corruption all about him swelled his sense of superiority and self-righteousness. The glaring humbug and hypocrisy that permeated his social environment was, however, more than he could long endure.

Having resigned his officer's commission he went abroad in 1857, to Switzerland, Germany, and France. The studies and observations made in these travels sealed his resolution to settle down for good on his domain and to consecrate his life to the welfare of his peasants. But a survey of the situation found upon his return made him realize that nothing could be done for the "muzhik" without systematic education: therefore, in order to prepare himself for efficacious work as a teacher, he spent some further time abroad for special study, in 1859. After that, the educational labor was taken up in full earnest. The lord of the land became the schoolmaster of his subjects, reenforcing the effect of *viva voce* teaching by means of a periodical published expressly for their moral uplift. This work he continued for about three years, his hopes of success now rising, now

Leo Tolstoy

falling, when in a fit of despondency he again abandoned his philanthropic efforts. About this time, 1862, he married Sophia Andreyevna Behrs, the daughter of a Moscow physician. With characteristic honesty he forced his private diary on his fiancée, who was only eighteen, so that she might know the full truth about his pre-conjugal course of living.

About the Countess Tolstoy much has been said in praise and blame. Let her record speak for itself. Of her union with the great novelist thirteen children were born, of whom nine reached an adult age. The mother nursed and tended them all, with her own hands made their clothes, and until they grew to the age of ten supplied to them the place of a schoolmistress. It must not be inferred from this that her horizon did not extend beyond nursery and kitchen, for during the earlier years she acted also as her husband's invaluable amanuensis. Before the days of the typewriter his voluminous manuscripts were all copied by her hand, and recopied and revised—in the case of "War and Peace" this happened no less than seven times, and the novel runs to sixteen hundred close-printed pages!—and under her supervision his numerous works were not only printed but also published and circulated. Moreover, she managed his properties, landed, personal, and literary, to the incalculable advantage of the family fortune. This end, to be sure, she accomplished by conservative and reliable methods of business; for while of his literary genius she was the greatest admirer, she never was in full accord with his communistic notions. And the highest proof of all her extraordinary *Tüchtigkeit* and devotion is that by her common sense and tact she was enabled to function for a lifetime as a sort of buffer between her husband's world-removed dreamland existence and the rigid and frigid reality of facts.

Thus Tolstoy's energies were left to go undivided into literary production; its amount, as a result, was enormous. If all his writings were to be collected, including the unpublished manuscripts now reposing in the Rumyantzoff Museum, which are said to be about equal in quantity to the published works, and if to this collection were added his innumerable letters, most of which are of very great interest, the complete set of Tolstoy's works would run to considerably more than one hundred volumes. To discuss all of Tolstoy's writings, or even to mention all, is here quite out of the question. All those, however, that seem vital for the purpose of a just estimate and characterization will be touched upon.

The literary fame of Tolstoy was abundantly secured already in the earlier part of his life by his numerous short stories and sketches. The three remarkable pen pictures of the siege of Sebastopol, and tales such as "The Cossacks," "Two Hussars," "Polikushka," "The Snow-Storm," "The Encounter," "The Invasion," "The Captive in the Caucasus," "Lucerne," "Albert," and many others, revealed together with an exceptional depth of insight an extraordinary plastic ability and skill of motivation; in fact they deserve to be set as permanent examples before the eyes of every aspiring author. In their characters and their setting they present true and racy pictures of a portentous epoch, intimate studies of the human soul that are full of charm and fascination, notwithstanding their tragic sadness of outlook. Manifestly this author was a prose poet of such marvelous power that he could abstain consistently from the use of sweeping color, overwrought sentiment, and high rhetorical invective.

At this season Tolstoy, while he refrained from

following any of the approved literary models, was paying much attention to the artistic refinement of his style. There was to be a time when he would abjure all considerations of artistry on the ground that by them the ethical issue in a narration is beclouded. But it would be truer to say conversely that in his own later works, since "Anna Karenina," the clarity of the artistic design was dimmed by the obstrusive didactic purpose. Fortunately the artistic interest was not yet wholly subordinated to the religious urge while the three great novels were in course of composition: "War and Peace," (1864-69), "Anna Karenina," (first part, 1873; published complete in 1877), and "Resurrection," (1899). To the first of these is usually accorded the highest place among all of Tolstoy's works; it is by this work that he takes his position as the chief epic poet of modern times. "War and Peace" is indeed an epic rather than a novel in the ordinary meaning. Playing against the background of tremendous historical transactions, the narrative sustains the epic character not only in the hugeness of its dimensions, but equally in the qualities of its technique. There is very little comment by the author upon the events, and merely a touch of subjective irony here and

Leo Tolstoy

there. The story is straightforwardly told as it was lived out by its characters. Tolstoy has not the self-complacency to thrust in the odds and ends of his personal philosophy, as is done so annoyingly even by a writer of George Meredith's consequence, nor does he ever treat his readers with the almost simian impertinence so successfully affected by a Bernard Shaw. If "War and Peace" has any faults, they are the faults of its virtues, and spring mainly from an unmeasured prodigality of the creative gift. As a result of Tolstoy's excessive range of vision, the orderly progress of events in that great novel is broken up somewhat by the profusion of shapes that monopolize the attention one at a time much as individual spots in a landscape do under the sweeping glare of the searchlight. Yet although in the externalization of this crowding multitude of figures no necessary detail is lacking, the grand movement as a whole is not swamped by the details. The entire story is governed by the conception of events as an emanation of the cosmic will, not merely as the consequence of impulses proceeding from a few puissant geniuses of the Napoleonic order.

It is quite in accord with such a view of history that the machinery of this voluminous epopee is not set in motion by a single conspicuous protagonist. As a matter of fact, it is somewhat baffling to try to name the principals in the story, since in artistic importance all the figures are on an equal footing before their maker; possibly the fact that Tolstoy's ethical theory embodied the most persistent protest ever raised against the inequality of social estates proved not insignificant for his manner of characterization. Ethical justice, however, is carried to an artistic fault, for the feelings and reactions of human nature in so many diverse individuals lead to an intricacy and subtlety of motivation which obscures the organic causes through overzeal in making them patent. Anyway, Tolstoy authenticates himself in this novel as a past master of realism, particularly in his utterly convincing depictment of Russian soldier life. And as a painter of the battlefield he ranks, allowing for the difference of the medium, with Vasili Verestschagin at his best. It may be said in passing that these two Russian pacifists, by their gruesome exposition of the horrors of war, aroused more sentiment against warfare than did all the spectacular and expensive peace conferences inaugurated by the crowned but hollow head of their nation, and the splendid declamations of the possessors of, or aspirants for, the late Mr. Nobel's forty-thousand dollar prize.

Like all true realists, Tolstoy took great pains to inform himself even about the minutiæ of his subjects, but he never failed, as did in large measure Zola in *La Débâcle,* to infuse emotional meaning into the static monotony of facts and figures. In his strong attachment for his own human creatures he is more nearly akin to the idealizing or sentimentalizing type of realists, like Daudet, Kipling, Hauptmann, than to the downright matter-of-fact naturalists such as Zola or Gorki. But to classify him at all would be wrong and futile, since he was never leagued with literary creeds and cliques and always stood aloof from the heated theoretical controversies of his time even after he had hurled his great inclusive challenge to art.

"War and Peace" was written in Tolstoy's happiest epoch, at a time, comparatively speaking, of spiritual calm. He had now reached some satisfying convictions in his religious speculations, and felt that his personal life was moving up in the right direction. His moral change is made plain in the contrast between two figures of the story, Prince Andrey and Peter Bezukhoff: the ambitious worldling and the honest seeker after the right way.

In his second great novel, "Anna Karenina," the undercurrent of the author's own moral experience has a distinctly greater carrying power. It is through the earnest idealist, Levine, that Tolstoy has recorded his own aspirations. Characteristically, he does not make Levine the central figure.

"Anna Karenina" is undoubtedly far from "pleasant" reading, since it is the tragical recital of an adulterous love. But the situation, with its appalling consequence of sorrow, is seized in its fullest psychological depth and by this means saved from being in any way offensive. The relation between the principals is viewed as by no means an ordinary liaison. Anna and Vronsky are serious-minded, honorable persons, who have struggled conscientiously against their mutual enchantment, but are swept out of their own moral orbits by the resistless force of Fate. This fatalistic element in the tragedy is variously emphasized; so at the beginning of the story, where Anna, in her emotional confusion still half-ignorant of her infatuation, suddenly realizes her love for Vronsky; or in the scene at the horse races where he meets with an accident. Throughout the

[178]

narrative the psychological argumentation is beyond criticism. Witness the description of Anna's
husband, a sort of cousin-in-kind of Ibsen's Thor-
vald Helmer, reflecting on his future course after
his wife's confession of her unfaithfulness. Or
that other episode, perhaps the greatest of them
all, when Anna, at the point of death, joins together the hands of her husband and her lover.
Or, finally, the picture of Anna as she deserts her
home leaving her son behind in voluntary expiation of her wrong-doing, an act, by the way, that
betrays a nicety of conscience far too subtle for
the Rhadamantine inquisitors who demand to
know why, if Anna would atone to Karenin, does
she go with Vronsky? How perfectly true to life,
subsequently, is the rapid *dégringolade* of this passion under the gnawing curse of the homeless,
workless, purposeless existence which little by
little disunites the lovers! Only the end may be
somewhat open to doubt, with its metastasis of
the heroine's character,—unless indeed we consider the sweeping change accounted for by the
theory of duplex personality. She herself believes
that there are two quite different women alive in
her, the one steadfastly loyal to her obligations,

the other blindly driven into sin by the demon of her uncontrollable temperament.

In the power of analysis, "Anna Karenina" is beyond doubt Tolstoy's masterpiece, and yet in its many discursive passages it already foreshadows the disintegration of his art, or more precisely, its ultimate capitulation to moral propagandism. For it was while at work upon this great novel that the old perplexities returned to bewilder his soul. In the tumultuous agitation of his conscience, the crucial and fundamental questions, Why Do We Live? and How Should We Live? could nevermore be silenced. Now a definitive attitude toward life is forming; to it all the later works bear a vital relation. And so, in regard to their moral outlook, Tolstoy's books may fitly be divided into those written before and those written since his "conversion." "Anna Karenina" happens to be on the dividing line.

He was a man well past fifty, of enviable social position, in prosperous circumstances, widely celebrated for his art, highly respected for his character, and in his domestic life blessed with every reason for contentment. Yet all the gifts of fortune sank into insignificance before that vexing, unanswered Why? In the face of a paralyzing universal aimlessness, there could be to him no abiding sense of life in his personal enjoyments and desires. The burden of life became still less endurable face to face with the existence of evil and with the wretchedness of our social arrangements. With so much toil and trouble, squalor, ignorance, crime, and every conceivable kind of bodily and mental suffering all about me, why should I be privileged to live in luxury and idleness? This ever recurring question would not permit him to enjoy his possessions without self-reproach. To think of thousands of fellowmen lacking the very necessaries, made affluence and its concomitant ways of living odious to him. We know that in 1884, or thereabouts, he radically changed his views and modes of life so as to bring them into conformity with the laws of the Gospel. But before this conversion, in the despairing anguish that attacked him after the completion of "Anna Karenina," he was frequently tempted to suicide. Although the thought of death was very terrible to him then and at all times, still he would rather perish than live on in a world made heinous and hateful by the iniquity of men. Then it was that he searched for a reason why the vast proportion of humanity endure life, nay enjoy it, and why self-destruction is condemned by the general opinion, and this in spite of the fact that for most mortals existence is even harder than it could have been for him, since he at least was shielded from material want and lived amid loving souls. The answer he found in the end seemed to lead by a straight road out of the wilderness of doubt and despair. The great majority, so he ascertained, are able to bear the burden of life because they heed the ancient injunction: *"ora et labora";* they *work* and they *believe.* Might he not sweeten his lot after the same prescription? Being of a delicate spiritual sensibility, he had long realized that people of the idle class were for the most part inwardly indifferent to religion and in their actions defiant of its spirit. In the upper strata of society religious thought, where it exists, is largely adulterated or weakened; sophisticated by education, doctored by science, thinned out with worldly ambitions and with practical needs and considerations. The faith that supports life is found only among simple folk. For faith, to deserve the name, must be absolute, uncritical, unreasoning. Starting from these convictions as a basis, Tolstoy resolutely undertook *to learn to believe;* a determination which led him, as it has led other ardent re-

Leo Tolstoy

ligionists, so far astray from ecclesiastical paths
that in due course of time he was unavoidably
excommunicated from his church. His convictions
made him a vehement antagonist of churchdom
because of its stiffness of creed and laxness of
practice. For his own part he soon arrived at a
full and absolute acceptance of the Christian faith
in what he considered to be its primitive and essential form. In "Walk Ye in the Light,"
(1893), the reversion of a confirmed worldling to
this original conception of Christianity gives the
story of the writer's own change of heart.

To the period under discussion belongs Tolstoy's drama, "The Power of Darkness,"
(1886).[1] It is a piece of matchless realism, probably the first unmixedly naturalistic play ever
wrought out. It is brutally, terribly true to life,
and that to life at its worst, both in respect of
the plot and the actors, who are individualized
down to the minutest characteristics of utterance
and gesture. Withal it is a species of modern morality, replete with a reformatory purpose that re-
flects deeply the author's tensely didactic state of
mind. His instructional zeal is heightened by intimate knowledge of the Russian peasant, on his

[1] The only tragedy brought out during his life time.

good side as well as on his bad. Some of his short stories are crass pictures of the muzhik's bestial degradation, veritable pattern cards of human and inhuman vices. In other stories, again, the deep-seated piety of the muzhik, and his patriarchal simplicity of heart are portrayed. As instance, the story of "Two Old Men," (1885), who are pledged to attain the Holy Land: the one performs his vow to the letter, the other, much the godlier of the two, is kept from his goal by a work of practical charity. In another story a muzhik is falsely accused of murder and accepts his undeserved punishment in a devout spirit of non-resistance. In a third, a poor cobbler who intuitively walks in the light is deemed worthy of a visit from Christ.

In "The Power of Darkness," the darkest traits of peasant life prevail, yet the frightful picture is somehow Christianized, as it were, so that even the miscreant Nikita, in spite of his monstrous crimes, is sure of our profound compassion. We are gripped at the very heartstrings by that great confession scene where he stutters out his budget of malefactions, forced by his awakened conscience and urged on by his old father: "Speak out, my child, speak it off your soul, then you will feel easier."

"The Power of Darkness" was given its counterpart in the satirical comedy, "Fruits of Culture," (1889). The wickedness of refined society is more mercilessly excoriated than low-lived infamy. But artistically considered the peasant tragedy is far superior to the "society play."

Tolstoy was a pessimist both by temperament and philosophical persuasion. This is made manifest among other things by the prominent place which the idea of Death occupies in his writings. His feelings are expressed with striking simplicity by one of the principal characters in "War and Peace": "One must often think of death, so that it may lose its terrors for us, cease to be an enemy, and become on the contrary a friend that delivers us from this life of miseries." Still, in Tolstoy's stories, death, as a rule, is a haunting spectre. This conception comes to the fore even long after his conversion in a story like "Master and Man." Throughout his literary activity it has an obsessive hold on his mind. Even the shadowing of the animal mind by the ubiquitous spectre gives rise to a story: "Cholstomjer, The Story of a

Horse," (1861), and in one of the earlier tales even the death of a tree is pictured. Death is most terrifying when, denuded of its heroic embellishments in battle pieces such as "The Death of a Soldier" ("Sebastopol") or the description of Prince Andrey's death in "War and Peace," it is exposed in all its bare and grim loathsomeness. Such happens in the short novel published in 1886 under the name of "The Death of Ivan Ilyitch," —in point of literary merit one of Tolstoy's greatest performances. It is a plain tale about a middle-aged man of the official class, happy in an unreflecting sort of way in the jog-trot of his work and domestic arrangements. Suddenly his fate is turned,—by a trite mishap resulting in a long, hopeless sickness. His people at first give him the most anxious care, but as the illness drags on their devotion gradually abates, the patient is neglected, and soon almost no thought is given to him. In the monotonous agony of his prostration, the sufferer slowly comes to realize that he is dying, while his household has gone back to its habitual ways mindless of him, as though he were already dead, or had never lived. All through this lengthened crucifixion he still clings to life, and it is only when the family, gathering about him shortly before the release, can but ill conceal their impatience for the end, that Ivan at last accepts his fate: "I will no longer let them suffer—I will die; I will deliver them and myself." So he dies, and the world pursues its course unaltered,— in which consists the after-sting of this poignant tragedy. ————————

Between the years 1879 and 1886 Tolstoy published the main portion of what may be regarded as his spiritual autobiography, namely, "The Confession," (1879, with a supplement in 1882), "The Union and Translation of the Four Gospels," (1881-2), "What Do I Believe?" (also translated under the title "My Religion," 1884) and "What Then Must We Do?" (1886). He was now well on the way to the logical ultimates of his ethical ideas, and in the revulsion from artistic ambitions so plainly foreshown in a treatise in 1887: "What is True Art?" he repudiated unequivocally all his earlier work so far as it sprang from any motives other than those of moral teaching. Without a clear appreciation of these facts a just estimate of "The Kreutzer Sonata" (1889) is impossible.

The central character of the book is a commonplace, rather well-meaning fellow who has been tried for the murder of his wife, slain by him in a fit of insensate jealousy, and has been acquitted because of the extenuating circumstances in the case. The object of the story is to lay bare the causes of his crime. Tolstoy's ascetic proclivity had long since set him thinking about sex problems in general and in particular upon the ethics of marriage. And by this time he had arrived at the conclusion that the demoralized state of our society is chiefly due to polygamy and polyandrism; corroboration of his uncompromising views on the need of social purity he finds in the evangelist Matthew, v:27-28, where the difference between the old command and its new, far more rigorous, interpretation is bluntly stated: "Ye have heard that it was said by them of old time, Thou shalt not commit adultery: But I say unto you that whosoever looketh on a woman to lust after her hath committed adultery with her already in his heart."

Now Tolstoy thinks that society, far from concurring in the scriptural condemnation of lewdness, caters systematically to the appetites of the voluptuary. If Tolstoy is right in his diagnosis, then the euphemistic term "social evil" has far wider reaches of meaning than those to which it is

Leo Tolstoy

customarily applied. With the head person in "The Kreutzer Sonata," Tolstoy regards society as no better than a *maison de tolérance* conducted on a very comprehensive scale. Women are reared with the main object of alluring men through charms and accomplishments; the arts of the hairdresser, the dressmaker, and milliner, as well as the exertions of governesses, music masters, and linguists all converge toward the same aim: to impart the power of attracting men. Between the woman of the world and the professional courtezan the main difference in the light of this view lies in the length of the service. Pozdnicheff accordingly divides femininity into long term and short term prostitutes, which rather fantastic classification Tolstoy follows up intrepidly to its last logical consequence.

The main idea of "The Kreutzer Sonata," as stated in the postscript, is that sexless life is best. A recommendation of celibacy as mankind's highest ideal to be logical should involve a wish for the disappearance of human life from the globe. A world-view of such pessimistic sort prevents itself from the forfeiture of all bonds with humanity only by its concomitant reasoning that a race for whom it were better not to be is the very one that will struggle desperately against its *summum bonum*. Since race suicide, then, is a hopeless desideratum, the reformer must turn to more practicable methods if he would at least alleviate the worst of our social maladjustments. Idleness is the mother of all mischief, because it superinduces sensual self-indulgence. Therefore we must suppress anything that makes for leisure and pleasure. At this point we grasp the meaning of Tolstoy's vehement recoil from art. It is, to a great extent, the strong-willed resistance of a highly impressionable puritan against the enticements of beauty,—their distracting and disquieting effect, and principally their power of sensuous suggestion.

The last extensive work published by Tolstoy was "Resurrection," (1889). In artistic merit it is not on a level with "War and Peace" and "Anna Karenina," nor can this be wondered at, considering the opinion about the value of art that had meanwhile ripened in the author.

"Resurrection" was written primarily for a constructive moral purpose, yet the subject matter was such as to secrete, unintendedly, a corrosive criticism of social and religious cant. The satirical connotation of the novel could not have been more

Leo Tolstoy

grimly brought home than through this fact, that the hero by his unswerving allegiance to Christian principles of conduct greatly shocks, at first, our sense of the proprieties, instead of eliciting our enthusiastic admiration. In spite of our highest moral notions Prince Nekhludoff, like that humbler follower of the voice of conscience in Gerhart Hauptmann's novel, impresses us as a "Fool in Christ." The story, itself, leads by degrees from the under-world of crime and punishment to a great spiritual elevation. Maslowa, a drunken street-walker, having been tried on a charge of murder, is wrongfully sentenced to transportation for life, because—the jury is tired out and the judge in a hurry to visit his mistress. Prince Nekhludoff, sitting on that jury, recognizes in the victim of justice a girl whose downfall he himself had caused. He is seized by penitence and resolves to follow the convict to Siberia, share her sufferings, dedicate his life to her redemption. She has sunk so low that his hope of reforming her falters, yet true to his resolution he offers to marry her. Although the offer is rejected, yet the suggestion of a new life which it brings begins to work a change in the woman. In the progress of the story her better nature gradually gains sway until a thorough moral revolution is completed.

"Resurrection" derives its special value from its clear demonstration of those rules of conduct to which the author was straining with every moral fiber to conform his own life. From his ethical speculations and social experiments are projected figures like that of Maria Paulovna, a rich and beautiful woman who prefers to live like a common workingwoman and is drawn by her social conscience into the revolutionary vortex. In this figure, and more definitely still in the political convict Simonson, banished because of his educational work among the common people, Tolstoy studies for the first time the so-called "intellectual" type of revolutionist. His view of the "intellectuals" is sympathetic, on the whole. They believe that evil springs from ignorance. Their agitation issues from the highest principles, and they are capable of any self-sacrifice for the general weal. Still Tolstoy, as a thoroughly anti-political reformer, deprecates their organized movement.

Altogether, he repudiated the systems of social reconstruction that go by the name of socialism, because he relied for the regeneration of society wholly and solely upon individual self-elevation. In an essential respect he was nevertheless a socialist, inasmuch as he strove for the ideal of universal equality. His social philosophy, bound up inseparably with his personal religious evolution, is laid down in a vast number of essays, letters, sketches, tracts, didactic tales, and perhaps most comprehensively in those autobiographical documents already mentioned. Sociologically the most important of these is a book on the problem of property, entitled, "What Then Must We Do?" (1886), which expounds the passage in Luke iii:10, 11: "And the people asked him, saying, What shall we do then? He answered and saith unto them, He that hath two coats, let him impart to him that hath none; and he that hath meat, let him do likewise." Not long before that, he had thought of devoting himself entirely to charitable work, but practical experiments at Moscow demonstrated to him the futility of almsgiving. Speaking on that point to his English biographer, Aylmer Maude,[1] he remarked: "All such activity, if people attribute importance to it, is worthless." When his interviewer insisted that the destitute have to be provided for somehow and that the Count himself was in the habit of giving money to beggars, the latter replied: "Yes, but I do not

[1] "The Life of Tolstoy," Later Years, p. 643 f.

imagine that I am doing good! I only do it for myself, because I know that I have no right to be well off while they are in misery." It is worth mention in passing that during the famine of 1891-2 this determined opponent of organized charity, in noble inconsistency with his theories, led in the dispensation of relief to the starving population of Middle Russia.

But in "What Then Must We Do?" he treats the usual organized dabbling in charity as utterly preposterous: "Give away all you have or else you can do no good." . . . "If I give away a hundred thousand and still withhold five hundred thousand, I am far from acting in the spirit of charity, and remain a factor of social injustice and evil. At the sight of the freezing and hungering I must still feel responsible for their plight, and feel that since we should live in conditions where that evil can be abstained from, it is impossible for me in the position in which I deliberately place myself to be anything other than a source of general evil."

It was chiefly due to the influence of two peasants, named Sutayeff and Bondareff, that Tolstoy decided by a path of religious reasoning to abandon "parasitical existence,"—that is, to sacrifice all prerogatives of his wealth and station and to share the life of the lowly. He reasoned as follows: "Since I am to blame for the existence of social wrong, I can lessen my blame only by making myself like unto those that labor and are heavy-laden." Economically, Tolstoy reasons from this fallacy: If all men do not participate equitably in the menial work that has to be performed in the world, it follows that a disproportionate burden of work falls upon the shoulders of the more defenseless portion of humanity. Whether this undue amount of labor be exacted in the form of chattel slavery, or, which is scarcely less objectionable, in the form of the virtual slavery imposed by modern industrial conditions, makes no material difference. The evil conditions are bound to continue so long as the instincts that make for idleness prevail over the co-operative impulses. The only remedy lies in the simplification of life in the upper strata of the social body, overwork in the laboring classes being the direct result of the excessive demands for the pleasures and luxuries of life in the upper classes.

To Bondareff in particular Tolstoy confessedly owes the conviction that the best preventive for immorality is physical labor, for which reason the lower classes are less widely removed from grace than the upper. Bondareff maintained on scriptural grounds that everybody should employ at least a part of his time in working the land. This view Tolstoy shared definitely after 1884. Not only did he devote a regular part of his day to agricultural labor; he learned, in addition, shoemaking and carpentry, meaning to demonstrate by his example that it is feasible to return to those patriarchal conditions under which the necessities of life were produced by the consumer himself. From this time forth he modelled his habits more and more upon those of the common rustic. He adopted peasant apparel and became extremely frugal in his diet. Although by natural taste he was no scorner of the pleasures of the table, he now eliminated one luxury after another. About this time he also turned strict vegetarian, then gave up the use of wine and spirits, and ultimately even tobacco, of which he had been very fond, was made to go the way of flesh. He practiced this self-abnegation in obedience to the Law of Life which he interpreted as a stringent renunciation of physical satisfactions and personal happiness. Nor did he shirk the ultimate conclusion to which his premises led: if the Law of Life imposes the

Leo Tolstoy

suppression of all natural desires and appetites and commands the voluntary sacrifice of every form of property and power, it must be clear that life itself is devoid of sense and utterly undesirable. And so it is expressly stated in his "Thoughts." [1]

———

To what extent Tolstoy was a true Christian believer may best be gathered from his own writings, "What Do I Believe?" (1884), "On Life," (1887), and "The Kingdom of God is within You," (1893). Although at the age of seventeen he had ceased to be orthodox, there can be no question whatever that throughout his whole life religion remained the deepest source of his inspiration. By the early eighties he had emerged from that acute scepticism that well-nigh cost him life and reason, and had, outwardly at least, made his peace with the church, attending services regularly, and observing the feasts and the fasts; here again in imitating the muzhik in his religious practices he strove apparently to attain also to the muzhik's actual gift of credulity. But in this endeavor his superior culture proved an impediment to him, and his widening doctrinal divergence from

[1] No. 434.

the established church finally drew upon his head, in 1891, the official curse of the Holy Synod. And yet a leading religious journal was right, shortly after his death, in this comment upon the religious meaning of his life: "If Christians everywhere should put their religious beliefs into practice with the simplicity and sincerity of Tolstoy, the entire religious, moral, and social life of the world would be revolutionized in a month." The orthodox church expelled him from its communion because of his radicalism; but in his case radicalism meant indeed the going to the roots of Christian religion, to the original foundations of its doctrines. In the teachings of the *primitive* church there presented itself to Tolstoy a dumfoundingly simple code for the attainment of moral perfection. Hence arose his opposition to the *established* church which seemed to have strayed so widely from its own fundamentals.

Since Tolstoy's life aimed at the progressive exercise of self-sacrifice, his religious belief could be no gospel of joy. In fact, his is a sad, gray, ascetic religion, wholly devoid of poetry and emotional uplift. He did not learn to believe in the divinity of Christ nor in the existence of a God in any definite sense personal, and it is not even

Leo Tolstoy

clear whether he believed in an after-life. And yet he did not wrongfully call himself a Christian, for the mainspring of his faith and his labor was the message of Christ delivered to his disciples in the Sermon on the Mount. This, for Tolstoy, contained all the philosophy and the theology of which the modern world stands in need, since in the precept of non-resistance is joined forever the issue between the Law and the Gospel: "Ye have heard that it hath been said, An eye for an eye, and a tooth for a tooth: But I say unto you, That ye resist not evil: but whosoever shall smite thee on the right cheek, turn to him the other also."

And farther on: "Ye have heard that it hath been said, Thou shalt love thy neighbor, and hate thine enemy. But I say unto you, Love your enemies, bless them that curse you, do good to them that hate you, and pray for them that despitefully use you, and persecute you." . . .

In this commandment Tolstoy found warrant for unswerving forbearance toward every species of private and corporate aggression. Offenders against individuals or the commonwealth deserve nothing but pity. Prisons should be abolished and criminals never punished. Tolstoy went so far as to declare that even if he saw his own wife or daughters being assaulted, he would abstain from using force in their defense. The infliction of the death penalty was to him the most odious of crimes. No life, either human or animal, should be wilfully destroyed.

The doctrine of non-resistance removes every conceivable excuse for war between the nations. A people is as much bound as is an individual by the injunction: "Whosoever shall smite thee on the right cheek, turn to him the other also." War is not to be justified on patriotic grounds, for patriotism, far from being a virtue, is an enlarged and unduly glorified form of selfishness. Consistently with his convictions, Tolstoy put forth his strength not for the glory of his nation but for the solidarity of mankind.

The cornerstones of Tolstoy's religion, then, were these three articles of faith. First, True Faith gives Life. Second, Man must live by labor. Third, Evil must never be resisted by means of evil.

Outside of the sphere of religious thought it is inaccurate to speak of a specific Tolstoyan philosophy, and it is impossible for the student to subscribe unconditionally to the hackneyed formula of the books that Tolstoy "will be remembered as perhaps the most profound influence of his day on human thought." Yet the statement might be made measurably true if it were modified in accordance with the important reservation made earlier in this sketch. In the field of thought he was not an original explorer. He was great only as the promulgator, not as the inventor, of ideas. His work has not enriched the wisdom of man by a single new thought, nor was he a systematizer and expounder of thought or a philosopher. In fact he possessed slight familiarity with philosophical literature. Among the older metaphysicians his principal guide was Spinoza, and in more modern speculative science he did not advance beyond Schopenhauer. To the latter he was not altogether unlike in his mental temper. At least he showed himself indubitably a pessimist in his works by placing in fullest relief the bad side of the social state. We perceive the pessimistic disposition also through his personal behavior, seeing how he desponded under the discords of life, how easily he lost courage whenever he undertook to cope with practical problems, and how sedulously he avoided the contact with temptations. It was only by an almost total withdrawal from the world, and by that entire relief from its daily and ordinary affairs which he owed to the devotion of his wife that Tolstoy was enabled during his later years to look upon the world less despairingly.

Like his theology, so, too, his civic and economic creed was marked by the utmost and altogether too primitive simplicity. Political questions were of slight interest to him, unless they touched upon his vital principles. If, therefore, we turn from his very definite position in matters of individual conduct to his political views, we shall find that he was wanting in a program of practical changes. His only positive contribution to economic discussion was a persistent advocacy of agrarian reform. Under the influence of Henry George he became an eloquent pleader for the single tax and the nationalization of the land. This question he discussed in numerous places, with especial force and clearness in a long article entitled "A Great Iniquity." [1] He takes the view that the mission of the State, if it have any at all, can only consist in guaranteeing the rights of every one of its denizens, but that in actual fact the State protects only the rights of the propertied. Intelligent and right-minded citizens must not conspire with the

[1] Printed in the (London) *Times* of September 10, 1905.

Leo Tolstoy

State to ride rough-shod over the helpless majority. Keenly alive to the unalterable tendency of
organized power to abridge the rights of individuals and to dominate both their material and spiritual existence, Tolstoy fell into the opposite extreme and would have abolished with a clean sweep
all factors of social control, including the right of
property and the powers of government, and
transformed society into a community of equals
and brothers, relying for its peace and well-being
upon a universal love of liberty and justice.

By his disbelief in authority, the rejection of
the socialists' schemes of reconstruction, his mis-
trust of fixed institutions and reliance on individual right-mindedness for the maintenance of the
common good, Tolstoy in the sphere of civic
thought separated himself from the political socialists by the whole diameter of initial principle;
he might not unjustly be classified, therefore, as
an anarchist, if this definition were neither too
narrow nor too wide. The Christian Socialists
might claim him, because he aspires ardently to
ideals essentially Christian in their nature, and
there is surely truth in the thesis that "every
thinker who understands and earnestly accepts
the teaching of the Master is at heart a social-

ist." At the same time, Christianity and Socialism do not travel the whole way together. For a religion that enjoins patience and submission can hardly be conducive to the full flowering of Socialism. And Tolstoy's attitude towards the church differs radically from that of the Christian Socialists. On the whole one had best abstain from classifying men of genius.

The base of Tolstoy's social creed was the non-recognition of private property. The effect of the present system is to maintain the inequality of men and thereby to excite envy and stir up hatred among them. Eager to set a personal example and precedent, Tolstoy rendered himself nominally penniless by making all his property, real and personal, over to his wife and children. Likewise he abdicated his copyrights. Thus he reduced himself to legal pauperism with a completeness of success that cannot but stir with envy the bosom of any philanthropist who shares Mr. Andrew Carnegie's conviction that to die rich is to die disgraced.

Tolstoy's detractors have cast a plausible suspicion upon his sincerity. They pointed out among other things that his relinquishment of pecuniary profit in his books was apparent, not real. Since Russia has no copyright conventions with other countries, it was merely making a virtue of necessity to authorize freely the translation of his works into foreign languages. As for the Russian editions of his writings, it is said that in so far as the heavy hand of the censor did not prevent, the Countess, as her husband's financial agent, managed quite skilfully to exploit them.

Altogether, did Tolstoy practice what he professed? Inconsistency between principles and conduct is a not uncommon frailty of genius, as is notoriously illustrated by Tolstoy's real spiritual progenitor, Jean Jacques Rousseau.

Now there are many discreditable stories in circulation about the muzhik lord of Yasnaya Polyana. He urged upon others the gospel commands: "Lay not up for yourselves treasures upon earth" and: "Take what ye have and give to the poor," and for his own part lived, according to report, in sumptuous surroundings. He went ostentatiously on pilgrimages to holy places, barefooted but with an expert pedicure attending him. He dressed in a coarse peasant blouse, but underneath it wore fine silk and linen. He was a vegetarian of the strictest observance, yet so much of an epicure that his taste for unseasonable dainties strained the domestic resources. He preached simplicity, and according to rumor dined off priceless plate; taught the equality of men, and was served by lackies in livery. He abstained from alcohol and tobacco, but consumed six cups of strong coffee at a sitting. Finally, he extolled the sexless life and was the father of thirteen children. It was even murmured that notwithstanding his professed affection for the muzhik and his incessant proclamation of universal equality, the peasantry of Yasnaya Polyana was the most wretchedly-treated to be found in the whole province and that the extortionate landlordism of the Tolstoys was notorious throughout the empire.

Much of this, to be sure, is idle gossip, unworthy of serious attention. Nevertheless, there is evidence enough to show that Tolstoy's insistence upon a literal acceptance of earlier Christian doctrines led him into unavoidable inconsistencies and shamed him into a tragical sense of dishonesty.

Unquestionably Tolstoy lived very simply and laboriously for a man of great rank, means, and fame, but his life was neither hard nor cramped. Having had no personal experience of garret and hovel, he could have no first-hand practical knowledge of the sting of poverty, nor could he obtain hardship artificially by imposing upon himself a mild imitation of physical discomfort. For the true test of penury is not the suffering of to-day but the oppressive dread of to-morrow. His ostensible muzhik existence, wanting in none of the essentials of civilization, was a romance that bore to the real squalid pauperism of rural Russia about the same relation that the bucolic make-belief of Boucher's or Watteau's swains and shepherdesses bore to the unperfumed truth of a sheep-farm or a hog-sty. As time passed, and the sage turned his thoughts to a more rigid enforcement of his renunciations, it was no easy task for a devoted wife to provide comfort for him without shaking him too rudely out of his fond illusion that he was enduring privations.

After all, then, his practice did not tally with his theory; and this consciousness of living contrary to his own teachings was a constant source of unhappiness which no moral quibbles of his friends could still.

Yet no man could be farther from being a hypocrite. If at last he broke down under a burden of conscience, it was a burden imposed by the

reality of human nature which makes it impossible
for any man to live up to intentions of such rigor
as Tolstoy's. From the start he realized that
he did not conform his practice entirely to his
teachings, and as he grew old he was resolved that
having failed to harmonize his life with his beliefs he would at least corroborate his sincerity
by his manner of dying. Even in this, however,
he was to be thwarted. In his dramatic ending,
still plainly remembered, we feel a grim consistency with the lifelong defeat of his will to
suffer.

Early in 1910 a student by the name of Manzos
addressed a rebuke to Tolstoy for simulating the
habits of the poor, denouncing his mode of life as
a form of mummery. He challenged the sage to
forsake his comforts and the affections of his
family, and to go forth and beg his way from
place to place. "Do this," entreated the young
fanatic, "and you will be the first true man after
Christ." With his typical large-heartedness, Tolstoy accepted the reproof and said in the course
of his long reply:[1] . . . "The fact that I am
living with wife and daughter in terrible and
shameful conditions of luxury when poverty sur-

[1] February 17, 1910.

rounds me on all sides, torments me ever more and more, and there is not a day when I am not thinking of following your advice. I thank you very, very much for your letter." As a matter of fact, he had more than once before made ready to put his convictions to a fiery proof by a final sacrifice,—leaving his home and spending his remaining days in utter solitude. But when he finally proceeded to carry out this ascetic intention and actually set out on a journey to some vague and lonely destination, he was foiled in his purpose. If ever Tolstoy's behavior irresistibly provoked misrepresentation of his motives it was by this somewhat theatrical hegira. The fugitive left Yasnaya Polyana, not alone, but with his two favorite companions, his daughter Alexandra and a young Hungarian physician who for some time had occupied the post of private secretary to him. After paying a farewell visit to his sister, a nun cloistered in Shamardin, he made a start for the Trans-Caucasus. His idea was to go somewhere near the Tolstoy colony at the Black Sea. But in an early stage of the journey, a part of which was made in an ordinary third-class railway compartment, the old man was overcome by illness and fatigue. He was moved to a trackman's hut at the station of Astopovo, not farther than eighty miles from his home, and here,—surrounded by his hastily summoned family and tenderly nursed for five days,—he expired. Thus he was denied the summit of martyrdom to which he had aspired,—a lonely death, unminded of men.

———

Even a summary review like this of Tolstoy's life and labors cannot be concluded without some consideration of his final attitude toward the esthetic embodiment of civilization. The development of his philosophy of self-abnegation had led irresistibly, as we have seen, to the condemnation of all self-regarding instincts. Among these, Art appeared to him as one of the most insidious. He warned against the cultivation of the beautiful on the ground that it results in the suppression and destruction of the moral sense. Already in 1883 it was known that he had made up his mind to abandon his artistic aspirations out of loyalty to his moral theory, and would henceforth dedicate his talents exclusively to the propagation of humanitarian views. In vain did the dean of Russian letters, Turgenieff, appeal to him with a death-bed message: "My friend, great writer of the Russians, return to literary work! Heed my prayer." Tolstoy stood firm in his determination. Nevertheless, his genius refused to be throttled by his conscience; he could not paralyze his artistic powers; he could merely bend them to his moral aims.

As a logical corollary to his opposition to art for art's sake, Tolstoy cast from him all his own writings antedating "Confession,"—and denounced all of them as empty manifestations of worldly conceit. His authorship of that immortal novel, "War and Peace," filled him with shame and remorse. His views on Art are plainly and forcibly expounded in the famous treatise on "What is Art?" and in the one on "Shakespeare." In both he maintains that Art, no matter of what sort, should serve the sole purpose of bringing men nearer to each other in the common purpose of right living. Hence, no art work is legitimate without a pervasive moral design. The only true touchstone of an art work is the uplifting strength that proceeds from it. Therefore, a painting like the "Angelus," or a poem like "The Man with the Hoe" would transcend in worth the creations of a Michael Angelo or a Heinrich Heine even as the merits of Sophocles, Shakespeare, and Goethe are outmatched in Tolstoy's judgment by those of

Prophets of Dissent

Victor Hugo, Charles Dickens, and George Eliot. By the force of this naïve reasoning and his theoretical antipathy toward true art, he was led to see in "Uncle Tom's Cabin" the veritable acme of literary perfection, for the reason that this book wielded such an enormous and noble influence upon the most vital question of its day. He strongly discountenanced the literary practice of revamping ancient themes, believing with Ibsen that modern writers should impart their ideas through the medium of modern life. Yet at the same time he was up in arms against the self-styled "moderns"! They took their incentives from science, and this Tolstoy decried, because science did not fulfill its mission of teaching people how rightly to live. In this whole matter he reasoned doggedly from fixed ideas, no matter to what ultimates the argument would carry him. For instance, he did not stick at branding Shakespeare as an utter barbarian, and to explain the reverence for such "disgusting" plays as "King Lear" as a crass demonstration of imitative hypocrisy.

Art in general is a practice aiming at the production of the beautiful. But what is "beautiful"? asked Tolstoy. The current definitions he pronounced wrong because they were formulated from the standpoint of the pleasure-seeker. Such at least has been the case since the Renaissance. From that time forward, Art, like all cults of pleasure, has been evil. To the pleasure-seeker, the beautiful is that which is enjoyable; hence he appraises works of art according to their ability to procure enjoyment. In Tolstoy's opinion this is no less absurd than if we were to estimate the nutritive value of food-stuffs by the pleasure accompanying their consumption. So he baldly declares that we must abolish beauty as a criterion of art, or conversely, must establish truth as the single standard of beauty. "The heroine of my stories whom I strive to represent in all her beauty, who was ever beautiful, is so, and will remain so, is Truth."

His views on art have a certain analogy with two modern schools,— much against his will, since he strenuously disavows and deprecates everything modern; they make us think on the one hand of the "naturalists," inasmuch as like them Tolstoy eschews all intentional graces of style and diction; and on the other hand of the "impressionists," with whom he seems united by his fundamental definition of art, namely that it is the expression of a dominant emotion calculated to reproduce itself in the reader or beholder. Lacking, however, a deep and catholic understanding for art, Tolstoy, in contrast with the modern impressionists, would restrict artists to the expression of a single type of sentiments, those that reside in the sphere of religious consciousness. To him art, as properly conceived and practiced, must be ancillary to religion, and its proper gauge is the measure of its agreement with accepted moral teachings. Remembering, then, the primitive form of belief to which Tolstoy contrived to attain, we find ourselves face to face with a theory of art which sets up as the final arbiter the man "unspoiled by culture," and he, in Tolstoy's judgment, is the Russian muzhik.

This course of reasoning on art is in itself sufficient to show the impossibility for any modern mind of giving sweeping assent to Tolstoy's teachings. And a like difficulty would be experienced if we tried to follow him in his meditations on any other major interest of life. Seeking with a tremendous earnestness of conscience to reduce the bewildering tangle of human affairs to elementary simplicity, he enmeshed himself in a new network

Leo Tolstoy

of contradictions. The effect was disastrous for
the best part of his teaching; his own extremism
stamped as a hopeless fantast a man incontestably
gifted by nature, as few men have been in history,
with the cardinal virtues of a sage, a reformer,
and a missionary of social justice. Because of
this extremism, his voice was doomed to remain
that of one crying in the wilderness.

The world could not do better than to accept
Tolstoy's fundamental prescriptions: simplicity of
living, application to work, and concentration
upon moral culture. But to apply his radical
scheme to existing conditions would amount to a
self-stultification of the race, for it would entail
the unpardonably sinful sacrifice of some of the
finest and most hard-won achievements of human
progress. For our quotidian difficulties his example promises no solution. The great mass of
us are not privileged to test our individual schemes
of redemption in the leisured security of an ideal
experiment station; not for every man is there a
Yasnaya Polyana, and the Sophia Andreyevnas
are thinly sown in the matrimonial market.

But even though Tolstoyism will not serve as a
means of solving the great social problems, it sup-
plies a helpful method of social criticism. And its

[215]

value goes far beyond that: the force of his influence was too great not to have strengthened enormously the moral conscience of the world; he has played, and will continue to play, a leading part in the establishing and safeguarding of democracy. After all, we do not have to separate meticulously what is true in Tolstoy's teaching from what is false in order to acknowledge him as a Voice of his epoch. For as Lord Morley puts the matter in the case of Jean Jacques Rousseau: "There are some teachers whose distinction is neither correct thought, nor an eye for the exigencies of practical organization, but simply depth and fervor of the moral sentiment, bringing with it the indefinable gift of touching many hearts with love of virtue and the things of the spirit."